THE BRIDGESTON
NOR

GW00853294

The Bridgestone
Food Lover's
Guide to

NORTHERN
IRELAND

CAROLINE WORKMAN - JOHN McKENNA

ESTRAGON PRESS

First published in 2005
by Estragon Press
Durrus
County Cork
© Estragon Press

Text © Caroline Workman & John McKenna
The moral right of the authors
has been asserted

ISBN 1 874076 75 8

Printed in Spain by Graphycems

IN MEMORY OF
ROBBIE MILLAR

WRITTEN BY
CAROLINE WORKMAN & JOHN McKENNA

SPECIAL CORRESPONDENT: HARRY OWENS

PUBLISHER: SALLY McKENNA

EDITOR: JUDITH CASEY

ART DIRECTION BY NICK CANN

COVER PHOTO BY MIKE O'TOOLE

ILLUSTRATIONS BY AOIFE WASSER

WEB: FLUIDEDGE.IE

THE AUTHORS WOULD LIKE TO THANK
Pat Curran, Colm Conyngham, Des Collins, Nick
Cann, Margie Deverell, Noel Doran, Suzanne
Doran, Jilly Dougan, Walter Ewing, Frieda Forde,
Frank Hederman, George Lane, Carol McIlroy,
Lelia McKenna, Frank McKevitt, Mike O'Toole,
Miguel Sancho, Hugh Stancliffe, Ann Marie Tobin,
Barbara Workman, Jock Workman, Sacha Workman

Bridgestone is the world's largest tyre and rubber company.

• Founded in Japan in 1931, it currently employs over 100,000 people in Europe, Asia and America and its products are sold in more than 150 countries. Its European plants are situated in France, Spain, Italy, Poland and Turkey.

• Bridgestone manufacture tyres for a wide variety of vehicles from passenger cars and motorcycles, trucks and buses to giant earthmovers and aircraft.

• Many new cars are fitted with Bridgestone tyres during manufacture, including Ford, Toyota, Volkswagen, Mercedes and BMW. Ferrari and Porsche are also fitted with Bridgestone performance tyres as original equipment.

• Bridgestone commercial vehicle tyres enjoy a worldwide reputation for durability and its aircraft tyres are used by more than 100 airlines.

• In Formula 1 Bridgestone supply tyres to leading teams and drivers, including Ferrari and Michael Schumacher. Technology developed in the sport has led to increased performance and safety in Bridgestone's road tyres.

• Bridgestone tyres are distributed in Ireland by Bridgestone Ireland Ltd, a subsidiary of the multinational Bridgestone Corporation. A wide range of tyres is stocked in its 70,000 square foot central warehouse and its staff provide sales, technical and delivery services all over Ireland.

• Bridgestone tyres are available from First Stop Tyre Centres and tyre dealers throughout Ireland.

FOR FURTHER INFORMATION:

BRIDGESTONE IRELAND LTD

10 Fingal Bay Business Park
Balbriggan
County Dublin

Tel: + 353 1 841 0000
Fax: + 353 1 841 5245

websites:
www.bridgestone-eu.com
www.firststop-eu.com

• The Bridgestone Food Lover's Guide to Northern Ireland begins with the capital city, Belfast, and is then arranged alphabetically by county, so Antrim precedes Armagh, and Down and Fermanagh are followed by Londonderry and Tyrone.

• The Bridgestone Food Lover's Guides include specialist producers as well as places to eat, places to stay and the best places to shop throughout the province. Our system has simply been to discover those people whose work represents the best they can achieve, whatever they cook or produce, wherever they sell their produce.

• In the sixteen years since we began writing about Irish food, we have seen one major change in the way information is passed on to the customer – this is the use of websites.

• Websites are a tool in which places can bring the most up-to-date information right onto your desk, often including a booking service, and shopping on-line service.

• Accordingly, our first preference has been to list a website, and this listing works interactively with our own site, www.bridgestoneguides.com, which acts as a portal for the addresses of all the best food and hospitality industries in Ireland.

• Obviously not every establishment has a website – indeed many small food industries have yet to make this leap. Where this is the case we have always given contact telephone numbers. In addition to this, we have indicated whether a restaurant is a daytime restaurant, or one that opens for dinner in the evening, or both.

• We have omitted detailed listings of prices and opening times, because these change regularly, and an out-of-date listing is not a helpful listing.

• Where we know that an establishment does not take credit cards this is indicated in the text, but very many places do take credit cards, particularly the Visa, Access/Mastercard group.

• The contents of the Bridgestone Food Lover's Guide to Northern Ireland are exclusively the result of the editors' deliberations. All meals and accommodation were paid for, and any offers of discounts or gifts were refused. This is an independent, critical guide.

• Finally, we greatly appreciate receiving suggestions – and criticisms! – from readers, whose opinions are of enormous assistance to us when discovering new people and new places for future editions.

FOR MORE INFORMATION & UP-TO-DATE CHANGES GO TO:

www.bridgestoneguides.com

The Bridgestone Awards
LOOK OUT FOR OUR BRIDGESTONE AWARD PLAQUES

The people and the places described in the Bridgestone Guides are entitled to display the annual Bridgestone Award, as a symbol of their excellence, their commitment and their creativity. Some people are awarded them year after year and display them all proudly. Some people like to customise them with lavish colours. But, whatever they might do with them, displaying a Bridgestone Plaque is the surest sign of excellence that you can get in Irish food.

Shops, producers and restaurants that are featured in the Bridgestone Guide also display our awards on menus, fliers, signs, adverts etc. These are carefully monitored and are your guide to true quality in Irish food. In a world of too much choice, we hope these awards will help you to find the best foods in Ireland.

HOW TO USE THIS BOOK

The world of food writing and criticism is awash with stars and gongs and icons, as if the business of food was rigidly hierarchical, leading inexorably to some pinnacle occupied by one restaurant, shopkeeper or producer. Bunk! Food isn't like that. The perfect ham sandwich is as noble as the truffled lobster, so long as you make it with skill and passion. So, we have decided to be a little more oblique in this book, and have tried to recognise individuality, uniqueness, differentness, rather than hierarchy.

To celebrate the creativity of chefs, shopkeepers, wine merchants and other producers of food, we have created the award of being On Top of their Game, signalling that a person or a place is at a creative peak.

Being Worth a Detour means exactly what it says: these are people and places worth going out of your way to discover, explore and enjoy.

The Greek word authentes – "one who does things for him or her self" – is the source for our Authentic symbol, signalling those artisan producers who are the backbone of every creative food culture: local people making delicious local foods.

THE BRIDGESTONE FOOD LOVER'S

CONTENTS

BELFAST CONTENTS

the epicurean age begins...

The City Food & Garden Market

To take the pulse of the food culture of Northern Ireland, and to capture a snapshot of just how the people of Northern Ireland now consider their food culture, take a trip to the Saturday morning City Food & Garden Market in St. George's food market.

We have seen the market ebb and flow since it first emerged in late 1999, when we were involved in organising and orchestrating the opening weekend. There have been periods when there were lots of producers, and lots of customers. And there have been other times: "At one point, we were down to just six producers", recalls Trevor Barclay, a stalwart of the market since that first weekend, and a man whose pork and bacon business was given a lease of life by the chance to sell direct to his customers in St George's.

But, this Saturday morning, as Mr Barclay sets up his stall with its coffee machine (!) and his grill (!) and his pork fillets and packets of sausages and bacon, all made from his own landrace pigs, there is something else happening.

For one thing, even by 10am, the place is buzzing. It is obvious, if you are a student of how people behave in food environments, that a breed of early shopper exists for the Saturday market, the early-adapters and early-risers who are here to get exactly what they want before the crowds turn up, the folk who want to select the cream of the crop and get back to their kitchens to think about the weekend's cooking.

And so, as the coffee stalls are setting up and the crêpes batters are being mixed, there are already queues at Cheese Etc, Trevor Irvine's exemplary cheese stall, and a place where you will find the rarest farmhouse cheeses in Ireland (Poulcoin from County Clare, Tullynascreena from County Leitrim, to name but two). At Mullan's farm stall, there is a queue of folk for organic chickens and eggs, and egg boxes are being returned, and conversations about food and cooking are beginning – "That chicken takes less time to cook now because it's organic, as there's no water to cook off".

At Ann Stone's Millview Farm Organics, the food lovers grab gorgeous parsnips topped with healthy handfuls of leaves, and there are fresh strawberries in peak condition, and bags of mixed salad leaves, and blackcurrants to be made into cordial, and feathery scallions.

At the fish stalls, there are tourists (tourists!) taking pictures of one another, as fresh crabs try to crawl out of their boxes and as Asian customers weigh the dark-shelled lobsters. At Javaman, the queue of caffeine-deprived souls is growing. Dale Orr, at the Churchtown Farm stall, is saying to the vegetarian boyfriend of a carnivorous customer: "When you smell this cooking, you will want to eat it as well", but it's said without bravado, but with simple confidence.

Simple confidence. At then the moment of realisation comes: what you are seeing, in the behaviour of customers, in the animated babble of conversation and music, in the confident gait of the stallholders, is the beginning of Ulster's Epicurean Age.

There has always been great food in Northern Ireland, especially its breads and meats, its potatoes and fish. But there has never been great confidence about these foods. Of course, pioneering restaurateurs have realised for as long as 15 years that they have something special to work with – wonderful Bann silver eels; great beef; superb seasonal game, good vegetables.

But what impresses about the atmosphere in the St George's Market is the confidence of the customers. These people know exactly what they want. "I'm the only

BELFAST

meat eater, so it has to be right!", says the girlfriend choosing her frying steak from Dale Orr. But she could as easily be selecting some superlative Moyallon meats, or great pork from Brian Wallace's Culdrum Farm, or half a leg of burgundy-red lamb from Mullan's farm stall. You meet a food-loving friend – a quintessential early-adapter and early-riser – and she shows you her organic chicken, and a large piece of mature Coolea cheese from County Cork, and delicate organic beetroots caked in dark soil amidst a basket of bounteous goodness.

There is a food culture going on here. You can hear it in the conversations – "I found the Cuban roast a wee bit dark"; "Our eggs are part of the organic breakfast in Soul Food on the Ormeau Road" – and you can see it in the behaviour and the body language: a group of young women going wide-eyed as the chilli bite of Sheila Keiro's Oliesto Foods tapenade kicks into their throats; the banter in the queue at Moyallon Foods – "Pay no attention to her, I know what I want" – the relaxed demeanour as children sit down with crêpess from La Creperie and Flour as their parents grab a Mossbrook Farm sausage butty and an Americano coffee.

What is happening is proof of the statement from Eric Schlosser, author of the seminal book, *Fast Food Nation*, which is quoted on the banner at Moyallon Foods: "People can be fed without being fattened or deceived". But we can take Schlosser's prescription one step further. The fattening bit and the deception bit are absent here, but what is present is even more vital: the pleasure bit. "People can be fed with pleasure and delight, for both customer and producer" might be a good motto for the St George's market, for pleasure and delight are its signatures. The Epicurean Age has arrived.

· *Aunt Sandra's Candy Factory* Vividly colourful sweeties of every hue and cry.

· *Barnhill Apple Juice* Ken Redmond's lovely apple juices come plain and flavoured with all manner of fresh fruits.

· *S. D. Bell's.* Come on, it is finally time to shell out thirty quid for 100 grammes of China White tea. Why? Because you're worth it, of course! Superb freshly ground coffees and even a mug of java to go.

· *Cheese Etc* Join the (very long) queue to get farmhouse cheeses in superb condition from Trevor Irvine, including some that are almost impossibly rare.

· *Churchtown Farm* Dale Orr will be serving the fantastic meats from his organic farm in South Down.

· *Corry Lane Smoked Fish* The Westmeath smokery has a stall close by the entrance with loads of excellent smoked fish.

· *Country Harvest* A huge stall right in the centre of the market with everything from baby squid to venison.

· *La Creperie* Delightful sweet and savoury crêpes for kids of all ages.

· *Culdrum Farm* Brian Wallace's super organic foods are brought from his own farm.

· *Drumgooland Smokehouse* County Down's artisan smokehouse has lots of great smoked foods and lots of exciting dressings and relishes.

· *Flour* The cult city-centre crêperie quickly builds up a long queue for imaginatively delicious crêpes.

· *Greenmount Meats* Look out particularly for the "salmon" cut of beef which is Dean Irwin's speciality.

· *Javaman* Superb brews from everyone's favourite coffee cart.

· *Miller's Traditional Bakery* Find the traditional breads of Northern Ireland, and don't miss the Belfast Baps sold at Marty Miller's bakery.

· *Millview Farm Organics* Ann Stone's organic produce draws a mega-queue early on, as the early-adapters get their hands on some ace organic fruit and vegetables from County Down.

· *Moss Brook Farm* Sausages and bacon to take home, and sausages and bacon in a big Miller's bakery bap from Trevor Barclay, a man who can manage half a dozen tasks at once.

· *Moyallon Meats* Jilly Dougan's extra-busy stall is where you will find rare-breed beef, lamb, pork and venison from one of the province's pioneering artisans.

· *Mullan's Farm* Superb eggs, organic chickens and lamb amidst other organic delights, all the way from Derry.

· *Offbeat Bottling Co.* Bangor's very own crafty condiment and preserve producer: the marmalades, in particular, have your Sunday morning toast calling out for them.

· *Olive Tree Company* All the way from the Ormeau Road with great Mediterranean specialities.

· *Oliesto Foods* Brilliant pestos and tapenades from Sheila and Hugh.

· *P & P Produce* Smashing fruit and veg from Philip McKee

· *Pheasants Hill Farm* Superlative rare breed meats from County Down.

· *Piece of Cake* Darko Markovic is a stalwart of markets from Belfast to Dublin, with excellent sweet and savoury baking.

· *Silverfin Fish Merchants* Excellent fish and shellfish from Ardglass, Kilkeel and Portavogie.

· *Souper Natural* Fine fresh soups

· *Windrush Foods* Wendy McGuire's Caribbean Cuisine food to go.

St. George's, Saturday, 10am-4pm. Live cookery demonstrations noon-2pm. Contact: Markets Section, Development Department, Belfast City Council, Cecil Ward Building, 4-10 Linenhall Street, Belfast
☎ 028-9032 0202, markets@belfastcity.gov.uk

City Centre/Bedford Street

Coffee Shop
● Clements Coffee Shop

Funky, functional design, characterised by rainbow-striped light boxes, low-slung, squishalicious sofas, and smooth iroko benches, is one of the key attractions of this successful home-grown coffee chain. They also serve consistently good Fair Trade coffees, sandwiches and a fine line of handcrafted, bought-in cakes and sweet tarts sold in substantial chunks and hunks that outlast a tall latte. Service accompanied by groovy tunes veers from slick to moody with a studenty crew, but their fierce individuality gives this chain its edge. (4 Donegall Square Wst ☎ 028-9024 9988; 66 Botanic Av ☎ 028-9033 1827; 37-39 Castle St ☎ 028-90434781; 342 Lisburn Rd ☎ 028-9068172; 131 Royal Avenue ☎ 028-9024 6016; Rosemary Street ☎ 028-9032 2293; 139 Stranmillis Rd ☎ 028-9020 1201 – Open day-time, Botanic and Stranmillis open late)

Café
● Cafe Renoir

The cakey, crusty wheaten bread and ruby raspberry jam that you get at CR are probably more homemade than your grandmother's. They also sell mountainous platters of filled baked spuds, toasties, and quiches heaped with salads kept fresh by a steady queue and a lively kitchen. Lots of sticky sweet things accompany mugs of tea keeping the sunshiny, stripped wooden room packed all day long. (5-7 Queen's Street, ☎ 028-9032 5592 – Open day-time)

Deli & Restaurant
● Deane's Deli

As we write, Michael Deane's deli is about to expand next door to have its own deli shop alongside the popular deli restaurant. The two stores have classy, elegant shopfronts, and graceful, spacious interiors. The deli concept is clever and simple; you can order small dishes at £5 – chilli chevre, for example, where a soft goat's cheese is wrapped in pancetta and served with salad leaves and a balsamic reduction, or grilled Portobello mushrooms with pastrami, basil aïoli and relish. This is nice, punchy, savoury cooking, and it's

BELFAST

served quickly so it's no wonder that the room is jammers at lunchtime. There are bigger dishes, such as bangers and mash or a navarin of lamb, with the daily specials chalked on the big blackboard. Espressos are excellent, staff are swift. (44 Bedford Street ☎ 028-9024 8800 www.deanesbelfast.com – Open day-time, Wed-Sat late)

Brasserie
● Deane's Brasserie

Michael Deane makes much of his new chef's experience with Heston Blumenthal, but happily the talented, modest Derek Creagh is steering clear of experimental, scientific cuisine, and is instead drawing on the invaluable principles and skills learned from English gastro-pubs and cheffy stars to produce some of the most lip-licking menus Deane's Brasserie has served in years. What's more, he's one of the few cooks innovating with local ingredients. Cured fillet of mackerel comes with escabeche and a tapenade crouton; chicken with creamed Savoy, macaroni, lardons and tarragon jus; cider braised belly of pork with langoustines, colcannon and clonakilty blackpudding; smoked cod with champ, parsley sauce and crispy pancetta. It's also great for light lunches, when soups – say, chilled tomato with crab and basil croutons – or tarts - lush, ripe tomatoes with a mellow, chive-flecked cod brandade, or Chulchoil goat's cheese with quince jelly, hazelnuts and organic leaves, are knocked out with the same panache. This is delicious, handsome, reasonably priced food that takes the focus off the giant cherubs and heavy-handed interior design, and has put the verve back into this downtown address. (38-40 Howard Street ☎ 028-9056 0000, www.deanesbelfast.com – open lunch & dinner)

Kitchenshop & Café
● Equinox

Kay Gilbert's gorgeous store has kitchenware and homeware that belong in the kitchen and the home of your dreams. In common with the other fine kitchenware and homeware stores of Northern Ireland, Equinox is distinguished by fastidious good taste: there is nothing in here that wouldn't congratulate your own aesthetic, whether you are buying some fab crockery or just a pair of slippers (the slippers, by Marimeko of Finland, are the business, incidentally). The little seating area for coffee and lunch at the rere of the store means you can spend hours in here in a state of blissful economic unconsciousness, purging your splurging with regular blasts of caffeine and some nice salads. (32 Howard Street ☎ 028-9023 0089 – open day-time)

Crêpess

● Flour Crêpe Room

A bijou, shoebox-sized bar with nifty design, a decent batter recipe and some sound menu ideas. Start with a savoury crepe, maybe mature cheddar, caramelised onion and thyme, and follow with something sweet, say Belgian chocolate and banana, or cinnamon stewed pear and apple (no whipped cream please, I'm being good). Then you'll feel like another savoury one - how about smoked salmon, crème fraîche, lime and chive? or Parma ham, Parmesan and rocket? And so it goes on, until, like the mirrored crêpe room, you'll be twice your normal size. (46 Upper Queen Street ☎ 028-9033 9966 – Open day-time)

Restaurant

● James Street South

On top of their game

BELFAST

Niall McKenna's restaurant is the epitomisation of the new Belfast Cool School. The bland exterior on a narrow alleyway conceals JSS's wowee! dining room, and the staff are just as cool as the classy, elegant, understated style. Mr McKenna's cooking is clean, precise and confident: Lough Neagh eel with capers, tomato and crisp salad leaves with a balsamic dressing has perfect balance and contrast between all of its elements; a pitch-perfect and painterly artichoke and tomato risotto is a truly great dish and shows utter mastery of the art of making the noble rice dish; a sublime lemon posset with berries and chantilly cream is superb nursery food made hip and trendy. The food in JSS looks every bit as good as it tastes, and it works because it isn't in any way fashionable; this style of cooking is beyond fashion, and has its own aesthetic. The punters who fill the place up at both lunch and dinner behave like a bunch of people who know when they are on to a good thing, and that good thing is the New Cool. Prices for such fine food aren't low, but they are keen. (21 James Street South ☎ 028-9043 4310 www.jamesstreetsouth.co.uk – open lunch & dinner)

only in ulster

wheaten bread

Northern Irish bakers say that wheaten, a bread made with any combination of brown or white flour, bicarbonate of soda and buttermilk, originated in Northern Ireland before it was adopted in the south. It goes back two to three centuries and today there are thousands of recipes on the same theme, each a jealously guarded secret learned from a grandma. From light and cakey to dark and nutty, it will be served to you for breakfast, and with soups, starters, and smoked salmon.

Home Bakery
● Millers Bakery

Fresh cut egg-salad sandwiches, sausage sodas, iced fingers, Paris buns, vegetable broth, Irish stew and cups of well-brewed tea are typical of the takeaway food produced by the busy outlets of this successful family-run home-bakery. Their moist, dense, nutty wheaten bread weighs a tonne and lasts all week, while the brioche-textured Belfast bap with its caramelised top and its fleeting freshness is excellent for immediate consumption.(64 Ann St ☎ 028-9031 3206; 18a Chapel Lane ☎ 028-9036 9393; Abbey Enterprise Pk, Mill Rd, Newtownabbey ☎ 028-9036 9393)

Café/Bar
● Nicholl's

A beautifully refitted café/bar in the heart of the shopping precinct, Nicholl celebrates the artist who once lived in this lovely remnant of old Belfast. In fair weather, they open the French windows, and chairs spill out onto the street. When it's chilly you make your way to the neat and cosy interior space where they serve decent daytime coffees, evening cocktails and lunchtime pub grub, such as pie and chips, warm potato salad with spicy Merguez, or a dry-aged rib-eye with béarnaise. (12-14 Church Lane, Belfast ☎ 028-9027 9595 – Open lunch & dinner)

BELFAST

Pizza Restaurant
● Pizza Express

See page 65. (25-27 Bedford Street, ☎ 028-9032 9050; 551
Lisburn Road ☎ 028-9068 7700 – Open lunch & dinner)

Restaurant
● Restaurant Michael Deane

Others have moved on from the classic, French-accented
dining experience which Michael Deane offers in the plush
upstairs space of his restaurant, preferring a more relaxed,
less intense dining experience. But Mr Deane remains true
to what some critics call a "fine dining" experience, by
which we understand an elaborate level of formality in both
service and cooking. Mr Deane is a master of this detailed
production, having created a palette of exotic and original
dishes over the years to which he remains devoted, and we
salute his dedication to the classic cooking of the twentieth
century. (38-40 Howard Street ☎ 028-9033 1134
www.deanesbelfast.com – Open dinner Wed-Sat)

Restaurant
● Roscoff Brasserie

Roscoff Brasserie is the yin of Paul and Jeanne
Rankin's pair of Belfast restaurants, the other,
Cayenne, most assuredly being the yang. RB is
restrained and feminine, where as Cayenne is
active and masculine. It's a logical and fun
dichotomy, whichever one you choose, but if you do choose
the yin, then you will get a classically subtle room in the
brasserie style, with cooking straight out of the classical
canon: carpaccio of beef with celeriac remoulade and
Roquefort dressing; chicken and ham hock terrine; duck
breast with Puy lentils; lobster thermidor; tart de jour. What
Paul Rankin has done in RB has been to return to his Roux
Brothers (remember them?) roots, and he has done it in a
intellectually understanding and historically respectful way,
and delivered it with a finesse that is wholly winning. (7-11
Linenhall Street ☎ 028-9031 1150 – Open lunch & dinner)

Delicatessen
● Sawyer's Deli

Sawyer's is the epitome of the traditional deli. Every manner
of condiment, every style of packaged pasta, every Oriental
and Mediterranean speciality can be found here, and the

BELFAST

best fun of all is to hunt it down amidst this tiny labyrinth and tabernacle of a store (you could ask the ever-helpful staff, but that would spoil the pursuit). For many, it is the wet fish counter and the fruit and veg that makes Sawyer's such a key city address, but however you use it, this is one of Belfast's icon destinations. (Fountain Centre ☎ 028-9032 2021)

Shop & Café
● Smyth & Gibson

A shot of espresso, an almond croissant or a chocolate brownie, and a gaze at *The Guardian* for five minutes before you head back to the office: that is the S&G urban experience, and a damn fine one it is too. The little café is upstairs from the über-cool shirt shop, and it's always jammed with lawyers and other people who can afford S&G shirts. For lunch, bring on the smoked duck salad with couscous, parsley and sweet soy, or the smoked Gubbeen with sun-dried tomatoes and relish, and we will be happy as sandboys on a sunny day. (Bedford House, Bedford Street ☎ 028-9023 0388 – Open day-time)

Kitchenware & Homeware
● Still

Still is a great store for two very simple reasons: it has unpredictable and covetable things to buy for the kitchen and the home, and it isn't expensive. Whereas the bigger chain stores tend over time to become predictable and pricey, this punky address has intriguing gear, whatever it may be that you are looking for. A simple set of bowls, for instance? Then check out that fab Umbra range. Groovy lights, mirrors, kitchenware and furnishings? All here, with your name on them and staking a claim to your credit card. A fun place to shop, explore and discover. (Royston House 34 Upper Queen St ☎ 028-9023 0494 www.stillforlife.com)

Brasserie & Bar
● Ten Square Grill Bar

It's hard to be all things to all people, but the Ten Square Grill makes a good attempt at being a place where you can enjoy a breakfast meeting at 7.30am, a mid-morning coffee break during shopping, a business lunch, cocktails or a night out with live music. They make this mix of offers work by offering a simple menu, specialising in grills, mixed in a well-designed space with colonial influences that manage to be both calmingly cool, reassuringly cosy, and well-maintained, save for the overlooked bathrooms. (10 Donegall Square South ☎ 028-9024 1001 www.tensquare.co.uk)

Restaurant
● Zen Japanese Restaurant

A brave, serious and successful attempt to bring Japanese food culture to Belfast, Zen is the best place for a raw fish fix. Mouthfuls of creamy, translucent shrimp and tender purple-suckered octopus are served with a surprising variety of tuna and seafood on fresh, picturesque sashimi platters. Surf clam, crab roe, mackerel and sticky grilled eel are included in a more familiar roll call of seat-belted sushi. Generous and delicious maki, including the rich seaweedy and toasted sesame crunch of prawn tempura and avocado maki, and the crystalline batter of lotus root, aubergine or sweet potato tempura, also make for a hugely satisfying lunch, dinner or mid-afternoon experience, enjoyed with pickles, miso, and warmed sake. Chinese owned and business-like, Zen offers its fair share of less reliable fusion. And with stairs leading to a sunken tatami room, and beaded pillars of light providing a corridor to rotating booth tables, it also offers some frivolous, 007-style cocktail glamour. (55-59 Adelaide Street ☎ 028-9023 2244 – Open lunch & dinner)

Great Victoria Street

Restaurant
● Cayenne

Danny Millar's cooking in the groovy Cayenne is as post-modern as the design and style of this glamorous, artistically conceived space. Lamb chops are done Korean style, for example, and served with kimchee and roasted potatoes. Salt and chilli squid comes with Asian slaw and a pair of dipping sauces. Here and there dishes are delivered in classic format – basil and ricotta gnocchi is a textbook dish, for instance, served simply with roasted yellow tomatoes – but Cayenne's signature style, for the most part is iconoclastic, and we rather like the fact that they like to rip up the rule book and deconstruct their fave dishes. The restaurant itself has grown mightily in size over the years, which rather puts pressure on the staff on busy nights. (7 Ascot House, Shaftesbury Square ☎ 028-9033 1532 www.cayennerestaurant.com – Open lunch & dinner)

Kitchenware
● Chef's Shop

Extended and glamorised, and now sporting a welter of funky modern Aga cookers for sale, Vincent McKenna's shop is a vital destination for everything from knives to blow-out cooking ranges, with everything else in between. Don't imagine that it's a shop reserved for the professionals: ordinary decent folk will be helpfully assisted to get everything they need to get the pan on. (Bruce House, 29 Bruce Street ☎ 028-9032 9200 www.thechefshop.net)

Café & Juice Bar
● Ginger Café

The front room café of Ginger has a few tables and chairs and a groovy bar where you can take coffee and a cake or some really punky daytime eats: chilli chicken with noodles and mange tout; fish pie; tuna Niçoise; pork and leek sausages with mash and a red wine jus. Comfortably informal, it's a great space to pause and re-fuel when shopping in the city centre. (68-72 Great Victoria Street ☎ 028-9024 4932 – Open lunch)

Restaurant
● Ginger Restaurant

Simon McCance's cooking is like no one else's. His style is so original and so deft that he quickly made his name in a tiny room on the Ormeau Road, but the new city centre room means more folk can enjoy this singular and unique food. The best way to describe it is to say that McCance cooks the way he is: easy-going yet somewhat anxious; focused but not quite certain; un-selfconscious and transparent. Other cooks seem to put technique between you and the ingredients, but McCance just makes them sing all on their own: fried spiced squid is a dish everyone does, but his dish tastes different from anyone else's. Tempura of hake with a baby potato, green bean and ginger curry isn't a curry the way anyone else would do it, and who else would mix tempura with curry and make it such a riot of flavours? Soft centre chocolate cake manages to be light and complete without being in any way fussy or elaborate. There is an asceticism in this man's culinary aesthetic, and it makes for some of the best eating you can find in Ireland. The room is relaxed and user-friendly, staff are ace, value is great, and Mr McCance is set fair to be one of the stars of the younger generation. (68-72 Great Victoria Street ☎ 028-9024 4932 – Open dinner)

Restaurant
● Istana Malaysian Cuisine

This sparkling clean, modest canteen, with lilac walls, laminate floors and smattering of vivid acrylic landscapes has tasty food and a memorably convivial atmosphere. Photographically illustrated in full Technicolour splendour, the menus offer a typically Malaysian cross-cultural mix of Chinese, Thai and Indian cuisine. However, it is the Malay specials that make this restaurant truly unique. Start with the coconutty, turmeric-spiced Penang laksa, move on to golden grilled skate - marinated with lime, chilli and shrimp paste and heaped with soft fried onions - and finish with the amazing 'ABC', a multicoloured bombe of tropical fruits, agar jelly, crushed ice and toffee-sweet cream. (127 Great Victoria Street, ☎ 028-9032 2311 – Open lunch & dinner)

Diner
● Rain City

A fresh, clean fuss-free diner, good for brunching, young families, and large party outings, Rain City also has a surprisingly large sun terrace and two coveted bay windows for al fresco dining when the rainy city allows. With chicken wings and nachos, T-bone steaks and club sandwiches, baked cheesecakes and cocktails, its menu has a strong mainstream American slant. However, if burgers and burritos aren't your thing then look more closely and you will find Rain City lite, where the flair, imagination and more invigorating West Coast Californian influences of Rain City's masterminds, Paul and Jeanne Rankin, shine through. A delicate summer prawn salad comes with waxy new potatoes, green beans and a chilly mayo. Thyme flavours a light chicken and porcini ragu served with orecchiette. Chickpeas, crushed with spices, contrast nicely with a crispy chorizo sausage. When the kitchen is up to speed, food is tasty, fast and fun. (33-35 Malone Road ☎ 028-9068 2929 – Open lunch & dinner)

Restaurant
● Suwanna Thai Restaurant

Suwanna is a busy, friendly neighbourhood-style eaterie, and hugely popular for cooking that pulls together Thailand's greatest culinary hits with other Thai favourites. (117 Great Victoria Street ☎ 028-9043 9007 – Open dinner)

Cathedral Quarter

Bagel Bar
● Bagel Bagel

BB is a key address for reliable tasty bagels, along with a range of melts, soups, coffees and cakes. The classic bagels such as chicken Caesar and their club are hard to get beyond, but there is much more to enjoy if you can drag yourself away from your faves and explore the full range of Joan and Paul Barr's fine concoctions. (60 Donegall Street ☎ 028-9024 2545 www.bagel-bagel.co.uk – Open day-time)

Wine Merchant
● Direct Wine Shipments

With half a century of trading safely under their belt, and with their wholesale operation now sold on, DWS seem as hungry as youngsters for the next stage of their history. With Peter McAlindon heading up their timeless Belfast store, the range of wines is quixotic and appealing, from terrific Spanish estates to gorgeous Soaves (believe it or not) to their traditional strong showing of clarets and New World wines. Over the last year more than 130 new wines have been sourced, part of what Peter McAlindon describes as "a new emphasis – an adventure to find new wines and new wines from new areas". Sometime soon there will be vintages available from the two estates the family own in Monsant and Priorat in Spain, and the progression from winesellers to winemakers will be one of the big wine stories of the next few years. In the meantime, there are fabulous bottles to be discovered, sold by people with a passion for what they do, and those setting out on the wine trail should note the exceptional emphasis on wine education which DWS has always espoused. (5-7 Corporation Square ☎ 028-9050 8000 www.directwineshipments.com)

BELFAST

Gastropub
● The John Hewitt

The JH was one of the first Belfast gastropubs, manned by a non-profit co-operative that has shown itself capable of firing out tasty modern food at crackingly keen prices. It's not always consistent, but when on form it's a great address. (51 Donegall Street ☎ 028-9023 3768 www.thejohnhewitt.com – Open lunch)

Restaurant
● Nick's Warehouse

Nick's Warehouse is a classic restaurant, a primal place, the stuff of our dreams and imaginings of what a restaurant should be, and how it should behave. The staff, for example, are simply the best, mixing formality with a genuinely friendly attitude to the customers. The food has remained at the sharp side of cutting edge for decades. The room is lovely, the wine list is aways amusing and well chosen, even the website is bloody impressive. What makes it so good? It is the sheer force of personality behind this establishment, specifically the richly cultured characters of Nick and Kathy Price. Mr and Mrs Price operate outside of the trivial fashions of the day, and they have always done this. It's no surprise that they should be such supporters of Slow Food, for what Slow Food does is simply to restate the primal principles, policies and philosophy of great food, and that, in effect, is exactly what happens in Nick's Warehouse every day.

So, it's lunchtime and what do you feel like eating? A piquant salad, perhaps embellished with Szechuan rare roast duck, or grilled sardines. (Go to the Anix.) Maybe something formal? Roast rump of lamb with parsnip mash and a mint butter sauce. (Yes! Go to the restaurant upstairs.) Now then, it's dinner. How about peppered goat's cheese mousse with an Italian Panzanella salad and a tomato dressing to start? Then might it be the Warehouse enchilada (butternut squash, chickpea and tomato) with melted cheddar, or grilled fillet of salmon with sticky coconut rice, dipping sauce and wasabi. And, if the principles of Nick's are primal, then the pleasures of Nick's are equally primal. (35-39 Hill Street ☎ 028-9043 9690, www.nickswarehouse.co.uk – open lunch & dinner)

BELFAST

belfast pubs

· *Apartment* Sprawl on sprawly sofas or bean bags and enjoy the view of Belfast City hall while you sup expertly made cocktails. (2 Donegall Square West ☎ 028-9050 9777 www.apartmentbelfast.com).

· *Bar Mono* There is nothing monochrome about Mono, an intimate wee bar with a jazzy soundtrack on the stereo. (100 Ann Street ☎ 028-9027 8886)

· *Café Vaudeville* Chandeliers, croissants and champagne cocktails are enjoyed from dawn until the wee small hours in the outlandishly extravagant and exuberant Café Vol au Vent, as it is known to locals. (25-39 Arthur Street, ☎ 028-9043 9160 www.cafevaudeville.com)

· *Crown Liquor Salon* An absolute jewel preserved by the National Trust. (46 Great Victoria Street ☎ 028-9027 9901, www.crownbar.com)

· *Cutter's Wharf* Take your drink outside and enjoy the energetic rowing teams on the Lagan. (Loughview Road, Stranmillis ☎ 028-9080 5100)

· The *Empire Music Hall* Comedy, salsa and Ken Haddock's supper club are what's on the menu in this old converted church, followed by a haddock supper from one of the chippers outside. (40-42 Botanic Avenue ☎ 028-9024 9276)

· *The Errigle* It's a pint of the black stuff for him and a brandy and ginger for the wife in the cosy fug of the wood-panelled Oak Lounge which dates back to 1735. (320 Ormeau Road ☎ 028-9064 1410)

· The *John Hewitt* Decent modern Irish pub grub, and regular poetry and pints are served in this city centre local, a repro bar whose friendly staff generate the spirit of a traditional bar. (51 Donegall Street ☎ 028-9023 3768, www.thejohnhewitt.com)

· *King's Head* A lavish, food-orientated conglomeration of

lounge bars and restaurants serving a particularly good selection of wheat beers. (829 Lisburn Road ☎ 028-9050 9950, www.kingsheadbelfast.com)

· *Madison's* Come here when you want to drink outside on sunny summer afternoons and mild nights. (63-65 Botanic Avenue ☎ 028-9050 9800)

· The high-tech, glass-fronted *Mercury Bar & Grill* is popular for jazz brunches on a Sunday afternoon. (451 Ormeau Road ☎ 028-9064 9017)

· *Nicholl's* A small, independent bar offering food, cocktails and cosmopolitan style. (12-14 Church Lane ☎ 028-9027 9595)

· *Northern Whig* A bold, brash café bar with typical modern pub grub, incongruous but attention-grabbing statues of Czech revolutionaries, and a few touchy feely soft furnishings. (2-10 Bridge Street ☎ 028-9050 9888, www.thenorthernwhig.com)

· *The Pot House* A gold fish bowl lit with a green haze where you can watch the people watching you through the glass floors and walls of this novelty bar. (1 Hill Street ☎ 028-9024 4044)

· *Ta Tu* An architecturally splendid, glamorous modern bar with outdoor decking, offering palatable grub until the dance music takes over later in the evening. (701 Lisburn Road ☎ 028-9038 0818, www.ta-tu.com)

· *Union Street Bar* A slick, lively, modern venue with brunches and saunas - the new heart of Belfast's burgeoning gay scene. (8-14 Union Street ☎ 028-9031 6060, www.unionstreetpub.com)

· *Whites 1630* Belfast's oldest tavern, sympathetically restored with simple whitewashed walls, stone flagged floors, scrubbed wooden tables, and a smoky peat fire. We can recommend the unchilled Guinness straight from the keg but not the food. (2-4 Winecellar Entry ☎ 028-9024 3080)

BELFAST

Laganside

Restaurant
● Bank Gallery Restaurant

Personnel changes in the kitchen have been taking place in the BG as we go to press, but the enjoyable room and the professional staff have been sailing through the changes with good grace, and the modern style of cooking they have established as their signature is unlikely to change. (The Edge, May's Meadow ☎ 028-9032 2000 www.at-the-edge.co.uk – Open lunch & dinner)

Restaurant
● Oxford Exchange Grill Bar

Dinner in the smart, glass-ceilinged Oxford Exchange can be something of a rollercoaster, with exquisite dishes succeeded by others that haven't been thought through. More simplicity should help to breed more consistency, for there is great potential here, and when the food hits the spot it can really shine. The room is at its best when the market below is in full swing, when the buzz of the traders and punters rises up to lift the mood of the place. (Unit 2, St George's Market ☎ 028-9024 0014 – Open lunch & dinner)

Market
● St George's Friday Market

The traditional Friday market in St George's is all things to all men. There are many brilliant food stalls, and cheek-by-jowl with these are many other stalls selling the most exquisite rubbish ever offered to man. We don't do exquisite rubbish in the Bridgestone guides, so we reckon you should focus on the good fish guys, like George S. Cully or S.P. Mulligan, buy some nice Suki tea, look out for Millar's Belfast Baps, get some nice muddy Comber queens, and stay far away from the guys who will sell you three sirloins for £5 or a copy of Ultravox's greatest hits on LP. The craic is always mighty. (St George's Market ☎ 028-9032 0202 www.belfastcapitalcity.com – Open 8am-1pm Fridays)

Market
● St George's City Food & Garden Market

See page 2. (4-10 Linenhall Street, Belfast ☎ 028-9032 0202, www.belfastcity.gov.uk – Open Saturday, 10am-4pm)

Restaurant
● **Tedfords**

Classic French training, and a ship-chandler's address, have both influenced Alan Foster's fish-focused, somewhat formal food offering. His ideas are sometimes elaborate and labour intensive, which can lead to disappointments if the kitchen is under pressure, or simply because, like the turbot with crab-crushed new potatoes, and grain mustard Hollandaise, the plates are over-complicated. Usually, however, Mr Foster's innovations are well judged and carefully handled. A stock-rich shellfish chowder is a fine starter, lightened by the aromatic freshness of its dill oil. Sweet roast scallops come with a smoky, creamed orzo of cod and broad beans, whilst pickled fennel cuts through a rich dish of salmon also served with a fennel purée. The room is attractive and comfortable, but it could do with more assertive service and funkier music. However desserts such as chocolate and hazelnut parfait and a passionfruit crème brûlée send the punters away with a positive impression. (5 Donegall Quay ☎ 028-9043 4000 – Open lunch & dinner)

The Gasworks/Donegall Pass

Homeware
● **Batik at the Gasworks**

June Elliott and her team have an eye for the classics of twentieth-century design, and in their new destination address Batik has the space to show off these droolsome design classics at their peachy, pristine perfection. If we won the Lotto, Batik would be the first place we would head to to disburden ourselves of the money, and you could not spend it on better furnishings: buying a Corbusier chair or a Richard Sapper light is the equivalent of buying a piece of art. Best of all, if it was in London or Dublin, a store with such implicit good taste as Batik would be staffed by frosty skinny girls dressed in black from tip to toe, but in Belfast Ms Elliott and her team make shopping a pure blast. Do be careful where you park, however, as keen prowling security guards in the Gasworks like to believe that they are acting in some dire Michael Bay movie. (Metter-Hoose Raa, The Gasworks ☎ 028-9024 9311 www.BATIKonline.co.uk)

Sandwich Bar
● The Gasworks Food Company

Carbohydrates abound at this sandwich, soup and scone café where specials of spicy bean burgers, falafel wraps, and focaccia melts are accompanied by helpings of cous cous, potato salad and coleslaw, rather than anything green. However most food is made on the premises and it's a good stop off for some thoughtful, tasty soups - potato and cheddar, cherry tomato & carrot, or porcini and Parmesan - or a reliable coffee and scone.(Unit 4B Cromac Quay, The Gasworks ☎ 028-9032 7474 – Open day-time)

Restaurant
● The Ginger Tree

Yes, it's the same people who used to persuade us all to trek to Ballyclare for Japanese food. They've gone for the same sense of serious, quiet, formality in their new urban space, kitted out in black table cloths, 80s chairs, and ornamental place-settings, and pleasant service is calm and ceremonial. The rather steeply priced food, from both the set and special selection menus, although tasty, can lack vitality and sparkle on quiet midweek nights. Still, you can sample a wide range of authentic specialities, from crisp-skinned pork tonkatsu with its fruity dressing, to sweet and salty kabayaki of Lough Neagh eel, dishes which make the GT well worth exploring. (23 Donegall Pass ☎ 028-9032 7151 – Open lunch & dinner)

Restaurant
● Sun Kee

The ethos of the ever-popular Sun Kee became more mainstream when it moved across Donegall Pass and opened up in the old Manor House Chinese restaurant. The b-y-o, minimalist ethic of the old room has been replaced by something much more in keeping with what many people expect of a Chinese restaurant: a large menu, staff in white shirts and ties and a familiar wine list. It remains a fun, friendly place to enjoy good Chinese cookery, effortlessly superior to the many other conventional Chinese restaurants in the city, and it continues to offer good value for money. (42-47 Donegall Pass ☎ 028-9031 2016 – Open dinner)

BELFAST

belfast chippers

· *The Bethany* A pristine red, white and blue colour scheme, and there is a sister branch on the Cregagh Rd. (246 Newtownards Rd ☎ 028-9045 4498)

· *Bishop's Restaurant* Bishop's is slick and busy, so don't expect speedy service. Slink into a booth and admire the gas fires, antique tiles, photos of Belfast and the traditional makeover. (30-34 Bradbury Place ☎ 028-9043 9070)

· *Fryer Tuck* Tuck into cod and chips made with the Fryer's special batter, and chips fried in dripping. (89 Bloomfield Rd ☎ 028-9047 1921)

· *The Golden Chip* The cognescenti rate the potato, onion and spice pasties. (12 Comber Rd, Dundonald ☎ 028-9048 0979)

· *Long's Fish Restaurant* Fantastic trad-style in Athol St, Long's do serious fish and chips. (39 Athol St, Tel: ☎ 028-9032 1848)

· *Manny's Carry Out* Seriously big portions are Manny's signature. (241 Antrim Rd ☎ 028-9035 1504)

· *Raffo's* Famous for their Belly Buster Burger, half a pound in weight! (174 Anderstonstown Road ☎ 028-9062 4854)

· *The Silver Leaf Café* Fresh fish and tasty, hand-made, traditional pasties. (15 Belmont Road ☎ 028-9047 1164)

· *The Sphinx Take Away Food Shop* Great felafel and real lamb kebabs, and a genuinely hot chilli sauce. (74 Stranmills Rd ☎ 028-9068 1881)

· *The Willow* A legendary chipper, established in 1921, and run by the Spence brothers, Bill and Martin. The Willow has a great community feel, and they wrap take-aways in newspaper! (52-54 Calvin St, Beersbridge Rd ☎ 028-9073 8808)

The University District

Bisitro
● Beatrice Kennedy

Refreshingly timeless, this cosy bistro with linen tablecloths and bentwood chairs is usually thronged with local residents. Situated right next to Queen's, it has the relaxed pace of the leafy city suburbs, although they also do a quick, brilliantly priced early bird menu for theatre-goers. Its capable chefs, Jim McCarthy & Tony O'Neill, have plenty of their own ideas, and food is tasty and prettily presented: a prawn and crab cocktail comes spiced with a crispy cool cucumber salad, or confit duck leg has a smart apple and fennel slaw. Then for mains, roast cod with caponata and basil beans, breast of chicken with lemony couscous, roasted peppers and a fiery harissa, or haunch of venison with spring cabbage and bacon, are served up with imaginative sides. Portions are generous but there's always room for a sticky toffee pudding or exotic fruity something or other, perhaps passion fruit mousse with pineapple and kiwi salsa. (44 University Road ☎ 028-9020 2290, www.beatricekennedy.co.uk – Open dinner & Sun lunch)

Café & Pizzeria
● Cafe Renoir

With acres of oak, architectural foliage, and earthy colours, this sharply designed, light-filled café and pizzeria is particularly alluring on cold nights when the warm glow and smoky aroma of its wood-fired oven beckons. It snuffs out any notion of hunger from the early morning – when luxurious porridge is topped with apple and cinnamon, or big breakfasts are made colossal with an optional slice of steak. For the rest of the day it does a brisk trade in sticky, sweet home-baked cakes and decent hot and cold sandwiches, pastas, and salads. In the evening the efficient self-service counter becomes a waiter station and you can pick your way through a sometimes daunting global selection to find a few gems, such as the Istanbul pizza of spinach, spiced roast aubergine, yoghurt and fresh parsley, or the lemon and garlic lamb cutlets served with a Greek salad. (95 Botanic Avenue ☎ 028-9031 1300. Also at 5-7 Queen Street ☎ 028-9032 5592, www.cafe-renoir.com – Open lunch & dinner)

Café/bar
● Conor Cafe Bar

This former William Conor art studio is a bright and airy space located opposite the Ulster Museum and Botanic Gardens in leafy South Belfast. Always busy, Conor offers a fair range of sweet things from huge cherry scones and traybakes to croissants and carrot cake, for tea and coffee breaks to be enjoyed around its large central table. Original salads such as the beetroot and roasted almond with yogurt dressing, or daily specials such as spiced duck breast, pepper a lunch and dinner menu of variable comfort food. Coffees are very good, and the small bar offers carefully selected wines and wheat beers. (11a Stranmillis Road ☎ 028-9066 3266 – Open lunch & dinner)

Canteen
● Great Hall Restaurant

See page 65. (Great Hall at Queens, Queens University, University Road ☎ 028-9024 5133, www.qub.ac.uk – Open day-time)

Restaurant
● Metro

An appealing seasonal menu in this smart, understated townhouse hotel offers tasty, quietly imaginative dishes that draw on global influences without ever being hackneyed. Steamed mussels, with a smoky sauté of chorizo, diced tomatoes and flat leaf parsley, or goat's cheese with lemon and pine-nut stuffed artichoke, drizzled with a sun-dried tomato vinaigrette, are typical starters and they are accurately delivered. Then come Indian spiced rump of lamb with aubergine purée and Indian mango salsa, or plaice paired with salsify, asparagus and new Comber potatoes. It's a far cry from the ciabatta, panini and burger lunch menu, although this too offers bribes such as steak and stout pie. What you get may, on occasion, not live up to the expectations raised by the menu, but the Townhouse is a good bet for a night out on Botanic Avenue, or if you don't feel like leaving the warm welcome of this pleasant, well-run hotel, whose location is a major asset as it puts you straight in the heart of the city.
(Crescent Townhouse, 13 Lower Crescent ☎ 028 9032 3349, www.crescenttownhouse.com – Open lunch & dinner)

BELFAST

Wholefood Shop

● Open Sesame

Helpfully open all hours in the heart of student land, this quirky, personal, well run independent health store provides an invaluable service to vegans, allergy sufferers and a community of careful consumers who need or fancy some sulphur-free dried apricots, organic oats, rooibos liquorice tea, fresh tofu and beansprouts, bio yoghurts, manuka honeys (good for stomach ulcers and arthritis as well as being much sweeter than ordinary honeys, the owner tells us), Green & Black chocolate ice cream, Honest cakes and cannabiscuits. A lot of happy customers, then. (32 Botanic Avenue ☎ 028-9032 4343)

Restaurant

● The Dim Sum Restaurant

Okay, so it's never going to be possible to get a table in Ferran Adria's El Bulli restaurant in Spain. So, what's the solution? The answer is to eat the fantastic dim sum in Oliver Tong's Dim Sum restaurant and, thereby, get yourself a blast of the ethereality, the textured surprise, the shock of the new, that Adria specialises in. And when you do have the fantastic dim sum, which this talented team confect, from sublime scallop dumplings, to pork intestine, to amazing satay tripe to the most ethereal beef rice rolls, you come to realise that what Ferran Adria is doing in El Bulli with European ingredients is nothing new, and that Chinese dim sum has always been about the exhilaration and delight of playing games with the textures and expectations of food. It's a pure thrill to eat here, and the secret to getting the best is to tell the charming waitresses that you want the dishes written in Chinese script at the foot of the menu, rather than the more conventional dishes concocted for conservative eaters. Quite simply ab fab. (82 Botanic Avenue ☎ 028-9043 9590 – open lunch & dinner)

only in ulster

vegetable roll

Well actually it's a roll or 'stick' of chopped, fatty meat
from the trimmings of brisket and rib with a seasoning of
fresh vegetables – usually celery, leek, carrot and onion,
in a synthetic casing - which is removed just before
cooking - and fried cut into slices. It was traditionally
part of an Ulster fry but is now more often served at
lunch or dinner with mashed potato or champ, and
mashed swede or turnip.

Ormeau Road

Asian Supermarket
● Asia Supermarket

Step into this cavernous store and warehouse on a Sunday afternoon, and you will
reckon they must be remaking Blade
Runner in Belfast in some new Steven Chow
movie, with the pulsing, seemingly chaotic energy of
the place threatening to tear it apart at the edges, as
the milling crowds hustle around, focused on getting the kai
lan and the beef brisket and the gourds and woks and the
whatever of ethnic cooking. It's wild and it's fun and it is not
to be missed, for not only is the choice extraordinary, but
the sheer energy of the place is nothing less than awesome.
By the second visit, you will be hooked. No other store in
Ireland has the sheer adrenaline rush of the Asia
Supermarket. (189 Ormeau Road ☎ 028-9032 6393)

Asian Supermarket
● The Balgla Supermarket

The Balgla is a newcomer to the Ormeau Road's pleasingly
polyglot mix of food stores. It has all the African and Asian
specialities you can imagine, as well as lots of interesting

speciality fruit and vegetables. Staff are friendly and witty –
"European customers wanted!" – and it's fun to detour in
here in search of something unusual.(175-177 Ormeau
Road ☎ 028-9033 1110)

Café
● Graffitti

Graffitti is a teeny-weeny, polka dot bikini of a neighbour-
hood café, whose homespun interior of glittering chandeliers and pastel-painted furniture attracts a local crowd in
search of decent food to consume with their BYOB wine.
While the sisters, friends and gap-year students run the
room, self-taught cooks manage the open galley kitchen.
Their homemade buxom beef burger served with chubby
chips is probably one of the best in Belfast. Try the generous
dishes of hot sticky chicken wings, marinated in chilli, car-
damom and honey, or goat's cheese, spinach and vine tomato tart, to be followed by stonking mains of salmon and
salsa verde or rib eye and garlic butter. And then, if you can
manage it, a wedge of homemade banoffee or lemon
meringue pie awaits. It's also an institution for brunch with
its trademark ciabatta fries, salami omelettes, and veggie
field mushrooms. (258 Ormeau Road ☎ 028-9069 3300 –
Open lunch & dinner)

Restaurant
● Macau

Macau is the most fun to be had in Belfast,
food wise. A tiny room halfway up the Ormeau
Road is home to the best staff and the best
buzz in the city and sitting here on any evening,
you are confronted by a simple fact: people,
people who have managed to get a table in Macau, are the
luckiest people in the world. And they know it.
So, what's to love? Well, for the McKenna children, bring on
the chicken and sweetcorn soup, the chicken chow mein;
the noodles with beansprouts and the beef with black beans
and green peppers (OK, so give the green peppers to the
old folks). For the McKenna parents, after they have
uncorked a bottle of BYO wine that helps to keep the cost
down, bring on the unctuous pork back ribs, the tangy hot
and sour soup, the perky scallops, the droolsome monkfish
and char siu hotpot, and the sparky, bright kai lan with ginger sauce. Fantastic service from Su-Ling and her team of

BELFAST

shirt-and-tie-smart waiters, a roaring buzz from the luckiest people in the world, and a tiny bill to which you add a whacking great tip. Thumbs up to Frankie in the kitchen, and book a table as you leave, if you want to once again be one of the luckiest people in the world sometime soon. (271 Ormeau Road ☎ 028-9069 1800 – Open dinner)

Greengrocer
● McCormick's Fresh Foods

Ricky Barrett's store is yet another of those fine fruit and vegetable shops that contribute to the brilliant neighbour-hood feel that you enjoy when shopping on the Ormeau Road. Friendly staff, lots of good fresh gear, an excellent deli counter, and an amiable, animated buzz at all times of the day are the splendid signatures of this fine store. (357-359 Ormeau Road ☎ 028-9049 1140)

Butcher
● Thomas McCreery's Butchers

McCreery's is a very stylish modern butcher's shop – it's even got an automatic door! – and alongside the good fresh meat there is a very popular hot food counter and good pies and bakes to take home. (439 Ormeau Road ☎ 028-9064 4911)

Butcher
● McGee's Butchers

Joe McGee's newest butcher's shop has cracking, state-of-the-art design, and a strong focus on staff training, coupled with an amazing choice of pre-prepared fresh meats. Mr McGee has no worries about playing David to the super-market Goliaths who are all around him - he knows they can't compete with him when it comes to expert butcher-ing and personal service. (Forestside Shopping Centre ☎ 028-9064 1116 www.mcgeesfood.com)

Greengrocer
● Michel's Fruit & Veg

There are a couple of excellent traditional fruit and veg shops on the Ormeau Road, and Michel's, opposite the Errigle, is one of them, with lots of good fresh veg arranged both inside and spilling splendidly and in an orderly fashion outside the store. (435 Ormeau Road ☎ 028-9064 2804)

BELFAST

Delitcatessan & Café
● Olive Tree Company

The Olive Tree started life as a stall in downtown Donegall Arcade and has since established its HQ on the up-and-coming Ormeau Road, as well as a regular pitch in St George's Market on Saturdays. Stocking the widest range of French and Italian olives in the city, The Olive Tree also offers lots of deli treats from excellent pesto (from imported gallon jars) to Roscoff-produced breads. The tiny six-table space upstairs is very popular with local gourmets, serving Illy coffee and fine patisserie, as well as all-day breakfast and daily soup, salad and pasta specials. Pasta might be warm fusilli with rocket, artichoke and Parmesan; salads are studded with Lombardi red peppers, smoked garlic and decent salami. It's hard to leave without investing in some baklava or dense brownies to take home. (353 Ormeau Road ☎ 028 9064 8898 – Open day-time)

Café
● Soul Food Company

Painted a Nigella blue, and decorated with naive and wonderful children's paintings, Soul Food is a fresh-faced family-run cafe serving mostly organic food. The menu is testament to cooks working hard to do the right thing. Until midday grilled Manx kippers come lavishly buttered with grilled tomatoes and chunky toasted wheaten, homemade muesli is served with yoghurt, or you can go for a grill of dry cured bacon, organic poached eggs, whole flat mushrooms and vine tomatoes, and still feel pretty virtuous. At lunch, pale yellow, egg-rich ravioli of spinach and ricotta are served with basil pesto cream and a snow of Parmesan, or sandwiches such as home-made hummus with aubergine chutney come in locally baked multi-seed rolls with dressed leaves. This leaves no time for baking but the handsome cakes (carrot, chocolate brownies) and sweet pies (pear and almond, rhubarb and apple) are welcome accompaniments for good coffees. (390 Ormeau Road ☎ 028-9064 6464 www.soulfoodco.com – Open day-time)

Wine Shop
● The Vineyard

Tony McGurran's small and perfectly formed wine shop is getting close to fifty years in business now, having crashed a bottle across its bow as long ago as 1957. It's a cracking

BELFAST

wine shop, but it is especially meritorious on account of the fantastic array of spirits they stock alongside the wine content. Just about every brew and hootch you can name is here, all sold with helpful charm. (375-377 Ormeau Road ☎ 028-9064 5774)

only in ulster

champ

A mashed potato dish made with milk and scallions, often enriched with butter, and sometimes with a beaten egg. You should serve it with a pool of melted butter swimming in a cradle on the top.

Lisburn Road

BELFAST

Delicatessen
● The Arcadia

Arcadia, like the equally long-established city centre shop Sawyer's, is one of those fab old-style Belfast delis, packed pell-mell to the rafters with lots of cheeses, speciality meats, salads and whatever-your-heart-desires. It never changes, and long may it stay that way. (378 Lisburn Road ☎ 028-9038 1779)

Asian Shop
● Camseng International Food Distributors

A good address for those in search of every manner of Asiatic specialities. (1 Lower Windsor Avenue ☎ 028-9066 9200)

Café & Delicatessen
● Cargoes

Way, way back in 1994, when we first wrote a piece of journalism about Cargoes, Mary Maw could say that "We feel we are doing missionary work", to describe what the Cargoes team was doing on the Lisburn Road – and had been doing at their previous Bloomfield Road address.

Back then that statement was true – Cargoes was years ahead of its time as a sleek, hip café and deli – but just look at how successful that missionary work has been. Mary and Rhada spread the gospel of good grub, and everywhere people shouted "Hallelujah!" and raised their forks to their lips. More than ten years on, Cargoes continues to do that missionary work, with unflagging faith in the gospel of great food, polite service, and delicious things to eat made with pride and care and reliable consistency. The ferment of culinary activity from the early 1990's that has created Northern Ireland's food culture has been enormously successful, and Mary Maw and Rhada Patterson are two of the leading lights in that cultural renaissance. We just wish they had time to do some more cookery books. (613 Lisburn Road ☎ 028-9066 5451 – Open day-time)

Butcher
● Coffey's

Coffey's is a pristine butcher's shop, with meats prepared with an exactitude that mirrors the meticulous and always-pristine state of the shop itself. Excellent sausages, great beef, lamb and pork, and lots of artfully prepared charcuterie, as well as a good service for game, explain its enduring success. (380 Lisburn Road ☎ 028-9066 6292)

Healthfood Shop
● Eatwell Health Foods

An excellent range of wholefoods and remedies – in particular sea vegetables – are the signature of Chris and Jim Hunter's popular wholefood store. (413 Lisburn Road ☎ 028-9066 4362)

Home Bakery
● June's Cake Shop

Like the many other traditional specialist bakeries that are such a fantastic feature of the Belfast food culture, June's is an invaluable address. Nothing here is modish or moody: it's simply a place for good Ulster baking, from soda farls to sweet buns to sausage rolls and fadge. There are nice sandwiches to be bought for lunch, and in an ever-changing world, June's rightly refuses to change. Amen to that. (376 Lisburn Road ☎ 028-9066 8886)

Greengrocer
● Mulholland's

The survival of the dedicated specialist fruit and vegetable shops in Northern Ireland isn't just some nostalgia trip on the part of Ulster punters. Shops like Mulhollands survive and thrive because they are superb at what they do: sourcing fresh local vegetables and fruit, and presenting and serving them with charm and skill, and leaving every supermarket offering in the shade by a million miles. Ace. (382 Lisburn Road ☎ 028-9020 2025)

Butcher
● Murphy's Butchers

Murphy's butchers has a cult following for its very fine steaks, and devotees will head to the top of the Lisburn Road to get strapping big doorsteps of dark red beef to bring home for the barbecue. (400 Lisburn Road ☎ 028-9068 2442)

Restaurant
● Shu

An old favourite since its previous incarnation as the Terrace, Shu restaurant has gone through several transformations and various chefs, whilst improving with age, experience, and the demands of local diners.

Alan Reid has always run a commercial operation, but now, with the arrival of Brian McCann in the kitchen, he is the proud owner of a destination restaurant that will raise the bar in Belfast.

Mr McCann has had lots of starry restaurant experience, but he has more than that in his repertoire. He is passionate, he understands seasonality, he has common sense and he is brimming with confidence and enthusiasm. A bright spark in the kitchen means Shu's menu is clever – but not clever-complicated. Instead McCann's food blows you away with its delicious, elegant simplicity.

Summery treats include a delicate herb salad with buffalo mozzarella, oven-dried cherry tomatoes, and salted almonds, or Glenarm salmon with steamed potatoes fennel and lobster sauce, or rump of lamb with potato fondant, artichokes, rosemary and balsamic jus.

A creamy smooth, voluptuously light foie gras and chicken liver parfait comes perfectly formed with freckles of fresh-

BELFAST

crushed white pepper, and a melt-on-your-tongue Muscat and camomile jelly. Crisped, firm, bright hake comes on a fine homemade tagliatelle with nutty, fried courgette, bursts of oven-dried cherries and a citrus gremolata. Macerated strawberries, in their own liquor served with a rich, fresh strawberry ice cream make a fitting end to a meal made with notably delicious ingredients and with a dexterous, light hand. Exciting stuff. (253 Lisburn Road ☎ 028-9038 1655 www.shurestaurant.com – Open lunch & dinner)

Café
● Swantons Gourmet Foods

Swanton's aims high with its extensive range of deli prod- ucts, from exotic jars of preserves to its own "Very Garlicky Pickle" and an admirable number of local and Irish foods can be found here.

They source good savouries such as spinach and feta filo pie, spicy potato cakes and tapenades, and make tasty soups, salad bowls and sandwiches – including pastrami, onion marmalade and the ubiquitous sunblush tomatoes, or Blacky ham, brie, and mango chutney. Plentiful salad garnishes come dressed in the lemony house vinaigrette. They open late on Fridays when you can BYOB. (639 Lisburn Road ☎ 028-9068 3388 – Open day time)

Sandwich Bar
● Tang Sandwich Excellence

Stephen and Jackie Friel's Tang has surely and steadily become one of the key destinations on the Lisburn Road, achieving the consistency and imaginativeness that distin- guishes the best places on this food lover's parade.

You can spot it a mile away, as it's brightly festooned with exaggerated-sized details of the awards their sandwiches have scooped over the years, and those awards are simply explained: excellent ingredients used with care and preci- sion and a real desire to elevate the art of the sandwich. Where else will you find yakitori chicken with spicy peanut sauce? Or Fermanagh black bacon with lettuce and vine- ripened tomatoes (now, that's how you make a BLT, we reckon). Or Belfast ham with roasted red pepper aïoli? These are sandwiches with big imagination.

"Fact: our food is unique", they assert confidently, and they may well be right. (625 Lisburn Road ☎ 028-9066 4451 – Open day-time)

BELFAST

Tapas Bar

● Taps

On weekend nights people queue here for a slice of the authentic tapas action that was missing from Belfast for so long, but they are also prepared to wait for the rare pressure-
free environment of a restaurant where second sittings and out times are never mentioned. Here you can graze for as long as you like on a succession of tasty morsels, or you can pop in for a speedy, light snack to quell an afternoon hunger pang. Citrus-marinated pork comes with a sauté of mixed bean, spinach, and roast pepper. Serrano ham on top of crusty bread carries fried quail's eggs sprinkled with Maldon salt. Aubergine & goat's cheese are wrapped and fried in crisp filo pastry and served with onion marmalade. Chicken is stuffed inside piquillo peppers and drizzled with pesto. And then there's the no less tempting gambas, patatas bravas, tortilla, and ensalada options before chunks of deep-fried crema Catalan chocolate cake, or pear tart. And all this for under £20. (479 Lisburn Road ☎ 028-9066 3211 www.tapswinebar.co.uk – Open daytime & dinner)

Noodle Bar

● Thai-tanic Noodle Bar

Framed Hokkien, vermicelli and flat rice noodles adorn the purple and orange walls of this friendly, family-owned noodle bar, where curry puffs, money bags, and satay skewers introduce a menu of surprising authenticity and variety. Dishes such as the chilli-littered Thai Beef salad, or the citrus, crushed-nut-laden Pad Thai, or the yummy coconutty Panang curry are permeated by the subtle, invigorating flavours of fresh herbs, lively spices and perky, vibrant veggies that you would not expect from a take-away. There are also a few sit-in bench spaces and outdoor café tables where the comings and goings of the take-away trade and the earnest staff provide in-house entertainment. (2 Eglantine Avenue ☎ 028-9066 8811 – Open dinner)

Greengrocer

● Whitten's Country Foods

Brian and Allen Whitten's amiable shop has nice fresh veg, which tumbles out onto trestle tables on the pavement. Look out for toffee apples, muddy spuds and leafy, stalks-on vegetables. (201 Lisburn Road ☎ 028-9038 2765)

BELFAST

Delicatessen

● **The Yellow Door**

Simon Dougan and his crew do great tasty food, and they do it with a rigour and a lack of pretension that is captivating. Like the best bakers and deli keepers, their work has a warm goodness, an holistic complexity and completeness, that seems to make buying a loaf of bread or a sandwich into something that is comforting and consoling, if not just downright life-affirming. Over the years, their confidence has grown, and with it the quality and completeness of the soups and pastries, the pies and bakes that they confect. Lovely cooking, simple as that. (427 Lisburn Road ☎ 028-9038 1961)

sweetie shops and ice cream parlours

· *Archie's/Desano's* Mrs Desano's shop is a classic, where they have been scooping out the cones and sliding out the sliders since 1938. The shop stays open 'until the ice cream runs out!' (344 Newtownards Road ☎ 028-9045 1608)

· *Vanilla's* Margaret Garland's sweetie and ice cream shop is a wee beauty. (131 Fall's Road ☎ 028-9031 0588)

· *Aunt Sandra's* There are warm, sugary aromas to be enjoyed in Jim and David Moore's sweetie factory, originally started by their Aunt Sandra. They make their own yellow man, fudge, nut brittles, candy shapes and boiled sweets, and buy in Belgian chocolates. Don't miss the "smelly feet"lollies! (60 Castelreagh Road ☎ 028-9073 2868)

· *The Chocolate Room* Christine Brittain makes a mean hot chocolate, as serious a hit of hot chocolate as you can get outside of Turin. Beautiful handmade chocolates from Ireland, Belgium, France and Germany are for sale. (529 Lisburn Road ☎ 028-9066 2110 & 23 Queen's Arcade ☎ 028-9032 0446)

East Belfast

Restaurant
● Aldens

Alden's offers a sublime restaurant experience, thanks to Cath Gradwell's inspired
cooking and Jonathan Davis's inspired man-
agement of this lovely room. It works as
well as it does because this pair have a natural generosity that sets the tone of this stylish,
confident space. The food is generous in flavour,
from classics like Dover sole with shellfish sauce to rabbit
stuffed with cotechino sausage to squid with black beans to
summer pudding, and no matter what she cooks, Ms
Gradwell manages to make something both utterly classical
and yet individually punky. Like the best female chefs, her
cooking isn't didactic: technique takes second place to a
very personal exploration of the culinary canon. Mr Davis,
meantime, is one of the great hosts, leading his team by gra-
cious example. Sublime. (229 Upper Newtownards Road
☎ 028-9065 0079 www.aldensrestaurant.com – Open lunch
& dinner)

Café and Bakery
● Amber's Humble Pie

We like Amber's. There isn't a whole lot to it – a room with
a gaggle of tables and chairs, a counter, laminated menus on
the tables, Dido on the sound system, a bakery out back,
and we wouldn't change a thing, save for the Dido. Locals
on the Holywood Road use it especially for their special
toasties, but any of the baking we have tried here is very
fine, thanks to using their own bread from the bakery. At
lunch they have ever-reliable specials such as steak and
onion special or chicken and ham special, along with paninis,
pasta salads, and with everything made on the premises –
something that is becomingly increasingly rare – quality and
flavours are spot on. (13 Holywood Road ☎ 028-9065 0111
– Open day-time)

Tea Room & Coffee & Tea Merchant
● SD Bells

You don't need to make your way up to the top

of the Newtownards Road to source Robert Bell's superb range of teas and coffees, for you can now get them at the St. George's Market on a Saturday, where you can buy a good brew to drink as well as everything from China White tea at £30 for 100grammes to San Agustin coffee. But, it is worth the trip to their shop to breathe in the creativity, the heritage and the striving for excellence that this firm embodies. Like the best food specialists in Northern Ireland, SD Bell's incorporates the intellectual and social culture of the products it sells, and has been doing so for over 100 years. Barry Bell is the roaster, and the Bell's guarantee is that coffee sold is ever more than 48 hours old, a vital consideration in creating a cup of coffee that delivers maximum satisfaction. But Robert Bell and his crew are equally passionate about their loose leaf teas, and everything they sell is distinct, and distinctively delicious. (516 Newtownards Road ☎ 028-9000 0000 www.sdbellsteacoffee.com)

Diner
● Bennett's of Belmont

Colleen Bennett really understands tasty food. At nine in the morning you can be munching away on a mushroom crostini with poached eggs in this excellent room, listening to Thin Lizzy or The Rolling Stones, and it's the sort of tactile experience that feels just right: urban, hip, and with just the right food and drink to make it a little special. The menu runs all day, and you can enjoy anything from an Ulster Fry to salmon with Bombay potatoes, aubergine and curry oil. Bennett's is both a savvy place – it's a totally cool room – and a sassy place, with great staff and a spot-on groove. (4-6 Belmont Road ☎ 028-9065 6590 – Open lunch & dinner)

Wine Merchant
● Compendium Wine Merchants

Putting together a case of wine in Compendium is just about the most vinous fun you can have. Get John and Neil to start talking about their newest arrivals, and suddenly half an hour has passed, you've actually assembled two cases of plonk, and you have also enjoyed an exhilarating wine lesson into the bargain. These guys know wine past and wine present – chardonnay is dead in the water; pinot gris is the next big white wine grape; the people of Belfast will pay any amount for good Kiwi sauvignon blanc – and

BELFAST

with the chat ranging from Txatkoli to Ernie Els to Osoyoos Larose from British Columbia, you feel that just by walking through the doors you have been taken all around the wine world in one lightning trip. Great wines, great service, but above all what you get at Compendium is all the fun and all the culture of wine. Smashing. (Alanbrooke Road, Castlereagh Industrial Estate ☎ 028-9079 1197 www.compendiumwines.com)

Bakery

● **Honest Wheatfree Products**

Rather than extracting the allergens and using the depleted remains of ingredients to make dry, 'funny-tasting' cakes with an edge of denial, Honest use whole, wholesome ingredients that naturally don't contain wheat or gluten. No nasties are added to the clever ground coconut, almond and rice combo: just lush fruits, nuts, chocolate, spices and zest. And they're handmade. Apricot and Cherry, Cranberry and Orange, Date and Pecan, Exotic Fruit, and Mocha are the current range. Definitely not just for coeliacs. Check out your local stockist at their website. (2 Woodstock Link, Belfast ☎ 028-9073 0166, www.honest.uk.com)

Home Bakery

● **Millers Traditional Bakery**

Miller's is both a food takeaway shop and a traditional bakery, near to the bottom of the Holywood Road, and you should look out in particular for their very fine wheaten bread, which has great lasting power, and the lovely Belfast Baps, which should be eaten asap. There are good soups and broths and hot and cold sandwiches and bacony-buttery sodas to buy to banish the hunger blues at mid-morning or at lunchtime. Nice friendly, sparky service. (23 Holywood Road ☎ 028-9020 7771)

Food shop

● **The Neptune**

A humble, crumbling shop furnished with lino and display fridges, strung with fishing nets, and selling all manner of salty sea snacks – dulse, winkles, potted herrings; and cooked poultry - roasted BBQ chicken, and chicken olives. It's also a popular destination for its pig's feet - steeped in salt and then boiled - a popular hangover cure, by all accounts. (310 Newtownards Road ☎ 028-9045 0542)

West Belfast

Fishmonger
● Walter Ewing

Walter Ewing is the big fish amongst fishmongers in Belfast, the man whose choice fresh fish is the first port of call for every self-respecting chef in the town and further afield. The shop itself is simple and pleasant, but its modesty will not alert you to the excellence of the fresh fish and shellfish that Mr Ewing always has on offer. And whilst you are in here picking up some sparky haddock or pristine prawns from the ladies behind the counter, then do try some of the smoked salmon that Mr Ewing smokes: it is very fine, with a distinctive, subtle taste palette that is most pleasing. (124 Shankill Road ☎ 028-9032 5534)

Butcher
● Owen McMahon Butchers

We first came across the splendiferous sausages made by Owen McMahon's team several years ago, at a tasting competition we were judging with chefs Nick Price and Noel McMeel. Amidst the stratospheric standards endemic amongst the best butchers in Northern Ireland, the McMahon sausages stood out as being particularly distinctive, showing the sort of deeply skilled charcuterie that is the hallmark of this Atlantic Avenue address. Alongside the excellent beef, lamb and pork there are lots of exotic meats also for sale. (3-5 Atlantic Avenue ☎ 028-9074 3525)

only in ulster

belfast ham

A Christmas-time treat, Belfast Ham is made with a leg of pork which is cured in salt for six weeks, and washed and dried, to be boiled and then cooked in the oven at home. Hundreds used to be made for Irish families living in England, and would be packed with salt in tea chests for the journey, but that trade has all died away, and Belfast ham is today extremely rare.

staying in belfast

· *Camera House* A pretty Victorian house that always enjoys excellent housekeeping, Camera House's Welly Park address gives it a serene location. (44 Wellington Park, ☎ 028-9066 0026)

· *Crescent Townhouse* The rooms at the front can be noisy on account of all the action on Botanic Avenue, but this is a comfortable and very well-located address. (13 Lwr Crescent, ☎ 028-9032 3349, www.crescenttown-house.com)

· *Malmaison* Malmaison did the expected Big Makeover when they moved to Belfas.t. Unfortunately, it was a Big Over-The-Top makeover, especially in the bar downstairs, which strains for effect and, failing to reach the correct effect, dies screaming in a sea of gloom. They just need to let some light in, and to copy more ideas from their Glasgow hotel, which is one of our favourites. (34-38 Victoria Street ☎ 028-9022 0200, www.malmaison.com)

· *The Merchant* Bill Wolsey's new hotel will, hopefully, be just the swish, svelte boutique destination, millions of visitors and tourists to Belfast will come to regard as their home-from-home. (Waring Street)

· *An Old Rectory* Mary Callan's house is especially renowned for a very fine breakfast, where no effort is spared to provide delicious alternatives to the fry-up. (148 Malone Road ☎ 028 9066 7882, www.anoldrectory.co.uk)

· *Ravenhill Guesthouse* Roger and Olivia Nicholson's guesthouse is restful and cultured, and run by the most helpful people. (690 Ravenhill Road ☎ 028-9020 7444, www.ravenhillguesthouse.com)

· *Ten Square* Fantastic location at the rere of the City Hall, and good bedrooms in this stylish complex. (10 Donegall Square, ☎ 028-9024 1001 www.tensquare.co.uk)

BELFAST

BELFAST

BELFAST

Ballycastle

Fishmonger
● Morton's

A popular local wet fish shop selling fresh fish from local waters as well as from County Down. (30 North Street, Ballycastle ☎ 028-2076 2348)

Delicatessen
● The Park Deli

A short stroll down from the main strip of Ballycastle, The Park is a useful stop for Segafredo coffee and is noteworthy as having a pretty good cheese counter, alongside a conventional counter with lots of cooked and salad ingredients, which they will helpfully pack into a baguette so you can feed your sand-scattered, wind-tousled kids. (5 Quay Road, Ballycastle ☎ 028-2076 8563)

only in ulster

yellowman
A golden confection, often confused with honeycomb, but similar in texture, sold at fairs and markets.

Butcher
● Wysner Meats

Wysner's is a more sedate shop today than several years back, and even in the peak of the Ballycastle summer it's a quiet retreat rather than a bustling busy business. But for their speciality black pudding, it is worth making the trip all the way up the coast, for this is a truly fine product, dotted with cubes of pork fat, the predominant scent a hit of cinnamon, and the texture is simply perfect. With the right energy behind it, Wysner's black pudding could be an icon product along the lines of Clonakilty black pudding. The family also operate a friendly café and upstairs restaurant immediately next door to the butcher's shop, with lots of domestically-inspired cooking in a cosy wee atmosphere. (18 Ann Street, Ballycastle ☎ 028-2076 2372)

Ballyclare

Organic Farm Shop
● Ballylagan Organic Farm

"I have dedicated my adult life to the search for idleness and I knew a farm shop would require an enormous amount of work," says Tom Gilbert, with his typical winning wit.."But I also enjoy producing and cooking and eating proper grub, and even on a small farm you can produce quite a lot. I also know there are quite a few people out there who can see through the supermarket cellophane, and past the cosmetic perfection of chemically produced food, to the more important issues of food quality. The questions I always ask myself are: does this contain anything that the human body is not evolved to digest? Does it contain anything that would have been unknown to my ancestors? At Ballylagan, we try to ensure that the answer to both questions is 'No, we only sell proper grub.'"

And the good news for those who seek proper grub is that this pioneering organic farmer has just received planning permission to build a new shop and butchery on the farm. No chance of any idleness for Mr Gilbert, then. (10 Ballylagan Road, Straid, Ballyclare ☎ 028-9332 2867 Open 2pm-6.30pm Thu, 9.30am-6.30pm Fri, 9.30am-5pm Sat, www.ballylagan.com)

Butcher
● Errol Jenkins Butchers

Errol Jenkins was one of the founding members of the Elite Butchers Association of Northern Ireland, a group whose standards manage to balance cutting-edge creativity with the wonderful ethos of the local shop selling local food to local people. But the significance of the Elite shops goes beyond their mastery of charcuterie, though that is profound, and is generally unmatched by other butchers on the island. What the Elite butchers have also managed to do is to become traiteurs for Northern Ireland, that is to say, cooked food shops as well as fresh meat shops. You will find people in Errol Jenkins shop buying food at lunchtime or food-to-go in the evening time who have probably never bought any fresh meat. Well if the Elite butchers can give these folk a better alternative to supermarket junk, saturated as it is with chemicals and produced by machines, then we reckon they should be acclaimed as saviours of the national and local diet. What you get in Jenkins', as in all the Elite shops, is skill, service, experience, and splendidly produced foods, from properly hung red meat to fantastic pies and even those favourites of kids of all ages: stuffed sausages. (41 Main Street, Ballyclare ☎ 028-9334 1822)

Ballymena

Artisan Cheese
● Causeway Cheese Company

Northern Ireland lags behind the republic when it comes to artisan cheese-making, although Damien and Sue McCloskey of the Causeway Cheese Company, who make the Cheshire-like Drumkeel in the shape of hexagonal causeway stones, are beginning to enjoy some recognition. Their cheese is exceptionally mild when it's very young, and the airtight wax covering does it few favours, but it benefits enormously from aging, so buy it from a reputable cheese-monger at about a year to 18 months old and you will discover a lovely cheese with a crumbly texture and an effervescent, buttermilky complexity.

You can also visit the plant to see cheesemaking in action, between April and September, but just call beforehand to make sure production is up and running. (Loughgiel Millennium Centre, Lough Road, Loughgiel ☎ 028-2764 1241 www.causewaycheese.co.uk)

Coffee bar
● Ground

This is the sister store to the Coleraine branch of Ground, and it's an invaluable address in Ballymena, easily outpacing the many other places to eat in terms of good food and a modish, pleasing style, with comfy sofas interspersed amidst the tables and chairs, and with sublimely enjoyable music playing. Good freshly roasted coffee, a pair of tasty soups at lunchtime and lots of nice sandwiches and wraps will make a day's shopping amidst the frock emporia of Ballymena all the better. (30-32 Ballymoney St ☎ 028-2565 0060 www.groundcoffee.net – Open day time)

Guesthouse
● Marlagh Lodge

All is cool, calm and comfortable at Marlagh
Lodge - after a mammoth two-year restoration
project on this gorgeous, sumptuous Victorian
listed building – and Robert and Rachel are
onto their next 'harebrained' scheme, they say,
running gourmet evenings with wine merchant James
Nicholson. Well actually we think it's a jolly sensible idea,
because as well as consummate musicians, interior design-
ers, and hosts, they're accomplished cooks. A sweet and
salty salad of roasted pears, Cashel blue and toasted walnuts, might be followed by fillet of beef with butter-roasted
shallots or a roasted red pepper, goat's cheese and poppy
seed tartlet. Refreshing summer desserts include a fresh
raspberry and blueberry jelly with mint cream. You can just
book for dinner party style eating. However, staying in
Marlagh Lodge's beautifully proportioned, exquisitely
detailed rooms, and Rachel's whiskey-laced tummy-warming
porridge, are indulgences you won't regret as your car tyres
crunch over the gravel. (Moorfields Road, Ballymena ☎ 028-
9443 3659, www.marlaghlodge.com)

Restaurant
● The New Manley

This is where well-informed locals go when they fancy a
spot of culinary chopsticks. Situated on Springwell Street,
just across from the car park and just down from the centre of town, it doesn't look like much, and the menu is typically lengthy and order-by-numbers, but it's the best-in-area.
(45 Springwell St ☎ 028-2564 8967– Open lunch & dinner)

Ballymoney

Preserves and Catering
● Causeway Chutneys & Minor Events

Next time you see a white Morris Minor
Traveller in the North Coast region, hail it
down as there's a good chance it will belong to
Virginia Maxwell, and she may just have a few
pots of her delicious homemade chutney in the boot. Made

in small batches with vegetables bought fresh from her local grocers, and wild fruits plucked from the hedgerows and trees, Virginia's sticky, sweet, fruity chutneys in ingenious combinations come in jars that you just can't leave shut for long. So, you'll be delighted to hear that as well as the small pots, she makes Kilner jars to order. Try the damson and cardamon chutney with game such as venison, or mature cheddar. Add a spoonful of the carrot and ginger with almonds to a vinaigrette, and serve the spiced apple chutney – studded with raisins - with a goat's cheese tart. The chutneys are on sale at the Osbourne family butchers in Ballymoney Main Street; Strawberry Fayre café, Coleraine; Jake Patterson's herb farm at Ballyvoy; the Causeway Cheese Company stand at St George's Farmers' Market, and they are available by mail order, direct from Virginia's kitchen, where she also prepares party food for her catering service, Minor Events. (19 Semicock Road, Ballymoney ☎ 028-2766 6394)

only in ulster

shortbread

Not just a Scottish speciality, butter-rich and melt-in-the-mouth shortbread is very Northern Irish – great with desserts such as rhubarb fool, or in front of the telly with a nice cup of tea. In fact, shortbread is so popular up here that they often use it as a base for other, richer tray bakes. The most popular of these is Millionaire's Shortbread – topped with both caramel and chocolate.

Ballyrobert

Restaurant
● **Oregano**
The positive feng shui of this country-side restaurant was inherited from the previous Japanese owners, and Dermot and Catherine Regan have sensibly just spruced it up with a new lick of paint, adding some modern Irish art and a modern Irish

menu. The friendly team is customer-conscious and interested in food. Homemade tagliatelle comes dressed with fresh chopped tomato, baby capers, radicchio, parsley, basil, and an unctuous extra virgin oil. Crab crème brûlée is a light, spiced, thickened cream topped with toasted sesame, and served with an Asian-edged sweet pickle dip and melba toast. The roast garlic risotto is good, teeming with wild mushrooms. A seared fillet of seabass is greatly enhanced with grassy, grilled asparagus, perky fresh apricots, waxy summer potatoes and a drizzle of olive oil. Desserts - poached peaches, pecan pie - aren't as strong - but they're homemade and seasonally inspired. (21 Ballyrobert Road, Ballyrobert ☎ 028-9084 0099 www.oreganorestaurant.co.uk – Open lunch & dinner)

Ballyvoy

Herb Garden & Café
● **Drumnakeel Herb Garden**

If you are circumambulating the north Antrim coast – and we definitely recommend that you do, for the vistas are splendid, the traffic is light, and the winding and steep coast road is exhilarating, albeit at times hair-raising – then look out for the sign on the main road and turn off and take a break at Drumnakeel, for a bowl of soup, a tuna melt, and the chance to browse amidst their herbs and plants whilst deciding what to buy to bring home from your day out. (Drumnakeel, Ballyvoy, Ballycastle ☎ 028-2076 3350 – Café open day-time, except Wed, Easter-end August; herb garden open Easter-end Sept)

Bushmills

Hotel & Restaurant
● **The Bushmills Inn**

Comfortable cooking, comfortable rooms and comfy-making open fires burning throughout the public rooms explain the success of the ever-popular Bushmills Inn. (9 Dunluce Road, Bushmills ☎ 028-2073 2339 www.bushmillsinn.com – Open lunch & dinner)

only in ulster

black bush

Just as we are about to go to press, it was announced
that Diageo – one of those global drinks groups with mul-
tiple "brands" in their portfolio – had agreed a £200 million acquisition of Bushmills. The parent company of
Bushmills, the French conglomerate Pernod Ricard, was
obliged to sell Bushmills because it was buying Allied
Domecq in another mega-buck takeover and makeover.
Such is the modern world of corporate drink brands.
Bushmills, it seems, is growing strongly as a brand,
especially in the United States, and Diageo wanted a
presence in this market, hence the complex chess game
of sale and purchase amongst global drinks giants.
There is another world to Bushmills, away from brands
and marketing and lifestyle advertising. Drinking a drop
of Bushmills can take you back in time as far as 1608,
when the first licence to distill was granted to Sir Thomas
Phillipps, deputy for the Plantation of Ulster. It was 1784,
however, before the Bushmills Old Distillery Company
was formed. We are particular fans of the splendid 10-
year-old single malt, but whiskey lovers really must try
the wild and wonderful Black Bush, a whiskey that is
unquestionably one of the finest blends in the world.

Distillery
● The Old Bushmills Distillery

The distillery tours organised and orchestrated by Irish
Distillers at its plants in Bushmills and Midleton, County
Cork, are really excellent tours, and normally we run
screaming from any manner of organised tourist escapade.
But seeing the process here, and tasting a dram or two,
really lets you know exactly how whiskey is made, and gives
you a taste for just how special a drink it is. Whiskey is a
magical liquid, created from a magical process, so do drop in
and see how the crack team at Bushmills make magic every
day. (Bushmills ☎ 028-2073 1521 www.bushmills.com)

Carnlough

Hotel & Restaurant
● **Londonderry Arms Hotel**

Waiters in bow ties, waitresses in skirts, sherries by the fire, and the quiet chink-chink of china in a carpeted dining room with white linen and country casual chairs are the initial signs of a rather predictable hotel à la carte roll-call of Galia melon, chicken liver pâté with buttered fingers of toast, prawn and Marie Rose cocktail, salmon with chive butter sauce, steak with sautéed onions and grilled tomato, and 'tempura' scampi with sweet chilli dip. It's not exactly a destination address, but this old-time coastal hotel is an attractive, comfortable stop-off if you are on the Antrim coast, and even if the food eschews fashion, it is hot, wholesome, and carefully prepared. (20 Harbour Road, Carnlough ☎ 028-2888 5255, www.glensofantrim.com – Open lunch & dinner)

Carrickfergus

Gastropub
● **Joymount Arms**

Sensible, smoke-free dining areas, fresh flowers, and gleaming wooden tables tell you that someone cares more than usual about the food being served in this pub, but you still won't be prepared for the flair and flavour of its menu if Johnny Ritchie is cooking. Leave room for the ambrosial rice pudding, or tip-top lemon tarts made by his brother, but it'll be difficult with the bold, comforting, Nigel Slaterish savoury dishes on offer. Chicken comes roast in lemon and thyme with spinach and ricotta tortelloni and a garlicky tomato sauce, or in a Maryland wrap with bacon, banana and blackened corn. Fish is beer battered and served with mushy peas, or seared, like the monkfish and served atop crushed spuds with a sage and Parma ham butter. Beef comes in a Guinness and mushroom pie with a butter pastry top or in home made lasagne with handcut chips and salad. Mighty food for mighty appetites. (16-18 Joymount Street, Carrickfergus ☎ 028-9336 2213 – Open lunch & dinner)

Cushendall

Potatoes
● Glens of Antrim Potatoes

Charlie McKillop's company is one of those all-too-few potato producing companies that have embraced both marketing and market research with assured intelligence. Their range of potatoes is excellent, and includes a fine range of organic potatoes, which they are continually developing. Whilst much production is sold via supermarkets' own-label brands, it is with their own GOA brand that we see a dynamic company moving away from the bland, commodity-minded mentality that has bedevilled potato growing in Ireland. To put it simply: we talk a good talk about how we value spuds, but we don't walk the walk, and the result is that we take the tuber for granted. GOA are showing how appreciation of potato varieties, and respect for the climatic and varietal aspects of potato growing, can make the humble spud anything but humble. (118 Middle Park Road, Cushendall ☎ 028-2177 1396 www.goapotatoes.co.uk)

only in ulster

steak & guinness pies

Steak and Guinness pie is the pub grub of choice in most parts of Ulster. The meat is cooked first, then a pie dish is lined with puff pastry, filled with the beef, then topped with the pastry. It differs from the UK pie, in that the pastry is both on top of, and underneath, the meat. Ulster pie-lovers regard the UK pastry-topped pie as a pudding. Butchers also sell a wide range of pies, with fillings such as mince and onion, or chicken and ham. These butchers' pies are usually made with shortcrust pastry – similar to the popular apple tart. This type of pastry, unlike puff pastry, holds together well and doesn't leak the contents.

Dunmurray

Restaurant
● H2O

It's hard to know why Martin Murray chose to have his restaurant in the shadow of Tesco in Dunmurray but neither H2O's inauspicious location nor the purple eighties' interiors seem to dissuade the swelling numbers of regular diners who come here to splurge their earnings on traditionally cooked roasts – bacon-wrapped, stuffed chicken, and kumquat and Cointreau glazed duckling; imaginative-cooking for vegetarians – a Stilton brulée comes with black olive crostini and caramelised red onion, cheese and parsnip roulade with sage and onion stuffing; and beat a culinary path for fish and game. Rabbit is cooked with bacon and button onions in chardonnay, wood pigeon comes with thyme jus and a honey and parsnip purée, lobster is halved and grilled with a simple garlic butter. Desserts range from Bramley apple crumble to baked Alaska, and fine cheeses echo the scope of the savoury menu, giving punters few excuses not to give H2O a go if they are in the area. (Kingsway House, Kingsway, Dunmurray ☎ 028-9030 9000 www.restauranth2o.com – Open dinner)

Glenarm

Organic Farmed Salmon
● Northern Salmon Company

Look out for the Glenarm salmon reared by the Northern Salmon Company in its beds just off the coast of this wee town. Many years ago we went out to see these beds, and were impressed by the massive currents of the sea, which meant the fish had to work super-hard, thereby developing musculature, and thereby developing flavour. Moving to organic certification was a smart move by Northern, for we know that the fish have not been doused with antibiotics and chemicals and have had plenty of space in which to swim in the pens. Northern is yet another of those visionary food companies whose pioneering techniques show how fish farming could and should be done. (Glenarm ☎ 028-2884 1691 northern.salmon@btclick.com)

Glengormley

Butcher
● The Quality Food Shop

Like all good butchers, David Thompson shows his mettle
by hanging his fine sirloins of beef for at least three weeks,
but that is merely one signature of a dedicated butchery
specialist whose shop exhibits all the careful hallmarks of a
member of the Elite Butchers Association. (7 Ballyclare
Road, Glengormley ☎ 028-9083 2507)

Lisburn

Brew Pub
● Hilden Brewing Company & Tap Room Restaurant

Hilden is both a bar and a brewing company, and for more
than 25 years Seamus Scullion has been the pioneer craft
brewer of Northern Ireland. You will find his ales – Hilden
Ale, Molly Malone and Great Northern Porter – for sale in
the bar, and in several other local pubs in the area. (Grand
Street, Lisburn ☎ 028-9266 3863)

Home Bakery
● Country Kitchen Home Bakery

Chris Ferguson's Country Kitchen is known for its butter-
rich shortbread and oat flakemeal biscuits, and you can find
all the traditional morning breads and a full range of wee
buns at his bakery counter. There is also a cosy tea room
for lasagne lunches, toasted sandwiches and Irish stew. (57-
59 Sloan Street, Lisburn ☎ 028-9267 1730 – Open
day time)

Portrush

College Canteen
● The Academy

Martin Caldwell oversees the restaurant at the Portrush
college, where students cook both lunch and four evening

dinners for guests. This is a splendidly ambitious venture, and one every food lover should try. The cooking is contemporary, if occasionally a little complex, but such is the permissible signature of youth. Full marks to the College for giving students the chance to perform in the real world before they go out into the real world. (Portrush College, Portrush ☎ 028-7032 3970 www.ulster.ac.uk/portrush/academy – Open lunch & dinner)

B&B
● Maddybenny Farmhouse
Rosemary White has made Maddybenny famous, thanks to her gargantuan B&B breakfasts, but the house nowadays is almost as well known for a popular equestrian centre that works alongside the B&B. (18 Maddybenny Park, Portrush, Coleraine ☎ 028-7082 3394)

Restaurants
● The Wine Bar, The Harbour Bistro, Coast
George McAlpin's Portrush empire has morphed into a series of smart fastish-food addresses, offering various spins on modern culinary icons such as pasta, pizza, burgers, chicken dishes and so on. If you have a bevy of kids on holiday in Portrush you will invariably make all three sites your own over the course of a week or two, and you will be impressed that fast food can be delivered with style and true flavours, not to mention such keen prices. Newer addresses in town such as 55 North have adopted elements of the cool modernism of the Wine Bar, but McAlpin remains ahead of the posse. (The Harbour ☎ 028-7082 4313 – Open lunch & dinner)

only in ulster

dulse

A salty, seaweed snack, originally harvested by fishermen to supplement their income when fishing was slack. Found at markets, and in some bars, it is also used in Robert Ditty's sesame seed and dulse oatcakes, and in the Causeway Cheese Company's cheese, and it can add a very pleasant saline edge to a loaf of soda bread.

Armagh

Café and Sandwich Bar
● The Bagel Bean

One of the few smoke-free zones in Armagh, Bagel Bean is a fresh, clean café and sandwich bar offering cappuccinos of a good strength, even if they are mug-sized, and a range of flavoured bagel sarnies and filled baked spuds made with real ingredients – field mushrooms, crisp grilled rashers, fresh mozzarella – instead of the pre-mix norm. There are a couple of interesting US ideas such as the peanut butter, cream cheese and banana combo, but most fillings are classics such as roast beef, iceberg and Dijon mustard mayo. Shakes, smoothies, brownies and wee buns are homemade too. (60 Lower English Street ☎ 028-3751 5251 – Open day time)

Café
● The Basement Cafe

Stuffed full of Holywood memorabilia, and families feeding their kids gravy chips and cowboy suppers of sausage, beans and chips, Margaret McCarthy's Basement might not look promising. However for every plate of chips there's a dish of Irish stew, made with chunky, tender ingredients, or a bowl of vegetable broth, teeming with just-cooked barley - both the better for a generous handful of fresh chopped parsley, and served with a big wedge of buttered bread and steaming mugs of tea. Homemade tray bakes follow, if you fancy something sweet. (Market Street, Armagh ☎ 028-3752 4311 – Open lunch & dinner)

Home Bakery
● The Cake Shop

Armagh's 50-year-old bakery encourages a strong home-baking and cake decorating tradition with its treasure trove of tins (for sale or hire), ribbons and cute cake decorations. Or you can be lazy and go home with bags of goodies, from whiskey fruit cakes, jam turnovers, and treacle tarts to the squares, pancakes, and potato cakes made with local apples. And that's just the sweet stuff. Pamela Johnston's cake shop is a good bet for picnic lunches if you touring this pretty town and its hinterland of fruit orchards. (20 English Street, ☎ 028-3752 2883)

Butcher
● A Flanagan & Son

David Flanagan's shop has been selling meat since 1931, proof – if any were needed – that the arrival of supermarkets in Northern Ireland has not merely not harmed the artisan butchers, but has in fact helped them to prosper in business and to bring on the next generation of skilled butchers and dedicated customers who know a good thing when they eat it. In common with most members of the Elite Association of Butchers, there is an impressive deli side of the operation, housed in a separate section, and with lots of good things to take home. Hunt down their own cured gammons, where the brining spices are prepared in house, and the meat cured for four days. Terrific beef is hung for three weeks, most of it is sourced from their own farm, from breeds such as Limousin and Blond Aquitaine. (1 Scotch Street, Armagh ☎ 028-3752 2805)

Restaurant
● Zio

Local staff greet their Sardinian colleagues with a 'Ciao' in this new branch of Zio, a group of modern Italian restaurants, which you'll also find in Derry, Banbridge and Belfast (sometimes under the Simply Italian brand). It's hard to rely on chains, and experiences seem to vary, but you can hit on a seam, as we did, of thin and crispy pizzas, or al dente pastas with fresh sauces, and there are no ill-conceived Italo-Irish concoctions. (7 Market Street, Armagh ☎ 028-3752 2220 – Open lunch & dinner)

only in ulster

potato farls

Dense, earthy flat bread, made with potatoes, flour, and buttermilk and cooked on a griddle. Potato farls can also be made as a turnover, stuffed with apples. They have a dappled brown surface that fries deliciously crisp in butter and are another essential element of a typical Ulster fry. They also toast well, to form a chewy crust which quickly melts butter into a rich, salty lava.

Craigavon

Tea Room & Pottery
● **Ballydougan Pottery**

See page 65. (Bloomvale House 171 Plantation Road ☎ 028-3834 2201 www.ballydouganpottery.co.uk – Open day time)

Artisan Charcouterie
● **Moyallon Foods Ltd**

It is more than a decade since Jilly Dougan first introduced wild boar to the family estate in Armagh, and since she first combined an interest in rare breeds with the practice of exemplary animal welfare. The outcome of such pioneering work has been the creation of speciality foods of superb, benchmark quality: wild boar; dry-cured saddleback bacon; Moyallon venison pies; wild boar and apple sausage; smoked chicken fillet, are all as good as it gets, and the sweetest bit is that the Moyallon range of meats are cheaper than the foods sold in the supermarkets. Every year brings a new clutch of gourmet prizes, and Mrs Dougan's real gift is that she can envisage a product as a total culinary whole, she thinks like an epicurean, which explains why the Moyallon range is just so satisfying and delectable. You could live on the Moyallon meat products and no other and never feel that you are missing out, such is their completeness and trueness. A true star. (The Farm, Crowhill Road, Craigavon ☎ 028-3834 9100 www.moyallonfoods.com)

Killeavy

Restaurant
● **Annahaia**

Annahaia is a beautifully designed moutainside restaurant, more-than-capably run by Ardal O'Hanlon, a bloke who likes to jet off to New York to catch up with the latest cocktail styles, and chef Michael Rath, who has just as much fun with a no-choice, seven-course menu as his partner does with the colourful drinks. Finely balanced and utterly delicious, the tasting menus generally comprise a well paced flow of dishes that leave you feeling refreshed and reinvigorated, rather than overstuffed. It might include a finely wrought tempura of fresh red mullet and spring onion with caponata, cous cous and sweet shrimp sauce; or piccata of veal, encased in a fine, nut-brown billowy batter, and served with a tumble of buttery, seasonal garden vegetables. Finish with desserts such as crème brulée with zappy ginger and rhubarb compote and then linger over coffees or wine with toe-tapping music in the cosy elegance of this gorgeous restaurant. Unfortunately, Mr Rath's time is divided between here and his Warrenpoint brasserie, but on good days and with this man in the kitchen, it is hard to find a better place to eat. (Slieve Gullion Courtyard, 89 Drumintee Road, ☎ 028-3084 8084 www.slievegullion-courtyard.com – Open dinner & Sun lunch)

Lurgan

Butcher
● John R Dowey & Son

John Dowey's shop is both butcher's shop and delicatessen, with many of the breaded and prepared products they make also sold as cooked and ready-to-go foods in the deli section. Excellent pies and fresh salads, and even organic fresh eggs, complete the picture of a shop that has all you need, backed up by informed expertise. (20 High St, Lurgan ☎ 028-3832 2547 jrdowey@aol.com)

Portadown

Artisan Cider
● Armagh Cider Company

Kelly Troughton's cider is made from their own apples and then processed in Hereford, in the UK, before making its way into local shops and bars. Carson's cider is a clear, modern cider, unlike the tradit-ional, cloudy farm ciders. Jilly Dougan of Moyallon Foods has used the cider to make a very delicious pork and cider sausage, and Ms Troughton's

company is a promising venture to watch out for.
(Ballinteggart House, 73 Drumnasoo Road, Portadown
www.armaghcider.com)

Apple Juice
● Barnhill Apple Juice

County Armagh is of course the orchard of
Northern Ireland, and Ken Redmond, a local
fruit farmer, grows over thirty varieties of eating
apple. Throughout the year he presses, blends
and bottles their juice to produce his wonderfully refreshing
and incredibly healthy range of apple drinks sold under the
Barnhill brand. The pretty pink and cloudy white juices
come laced with blackberries, blackcurrant, raspberries,
elderflower, and cinnamon, but even the simple flavours
offer an incredible variety of tastes throughout the year.
They always blend three or four varieties and every time
they'll be different. That makes each batch of juice unique -
it's part of the excitement of making and drinking Barnhill.
(Barnhill, Portadown ☎ 028-3885 1190)

Greengrocer
● Chapmans

Twenty-two staff members are employed and 40' containers
are a common sight at Chapmans, which opens its doors to
a continuous stream of County Armagh housewives. They
clearly like their greens. But it's not just super-fresh fruit
and vegetables in which the Chapman brothers excel. Bread
and pastries from Armagh bakers, locally-made salads and
ready meals, pre-packed sausages and prime cuts from local
butchers, jams and chutneys, frozen fruits and fruit juices
are all hoovered up with great gusto. (47 Dobbin Road
☎ 028-3833 2918)

Wine Merchant
● Ell's Fine Wine

Ell's is a very successful wine merchant, with over 700 wines
for sale, both in its retail and wholesale operations (the
wholesale side is dealt with as R&R Wines), and their areas
of expertise, such as Australia and Portugal, are unearthing
some star finds.
Look out also for fine sauvignons from New Zealand and
good-value wines sourced direct from France. (42 Dobbin
Rd, Portadown ☎ 028-3833 2306 rrwines@hotmail.com)

Butcher
● T Knox & Sons

Barry Knox prepares his beef the traditional way, boning it by hand in the shop, and it will have been hanging for all of three weeks before it is finally trimmed, sliced and presented for sale. But don't overlook their excellent prepared food, such as the wonderful pies – minced meat, steak, steak & kidney, to name just three – because they even make their own pastry for the pies, a move that is typical of the care shown in this shop. (388 West St, Portadown ☎ 028-3835 3713)

Charcouterie
● William Sprott Ltd

Founded by William Sprott in 1910, Sprotts are curers and producers of green and smoked bacon with good fat cover, crackling rind and robust, dense meat, supplied in muslin-wrapped sides to butchers, such as Orrs of Holywood, or sliced and packaged for local branches of the multiples. The secret is in their live brine, which they use for immersion rather than injection, and the traditional processes, which involve removing, rather than adding water. "You can write down what you do, a basic recipe, but there are a lot of things you can't write down. There are certain things built in. The curers don't know themselves. It's all done by touch and sight and a whole lot of intangibles that you can only pick up with time and experience," says general manager, Boyd Hunter. They also make traditionally cooked hams and dry-cured legs of pork – or Belfast Hams. Sprotts are one of only six members of the Ulster Curers Association, whose membership was in the 100s only 40 years ago. (Edward Street, Portadown ☎ 028-3833 2157)

Potatoes
● Wilsons Country Potatoes

You will find Wilson's potatoes almost everywhere, which is good news for food lovers as their spuds are uniformly excellent. Cleverly packaged, with details of the variety, and sold according to their culinary purpose, they are a beacon for other potato producers who are still stuck in the days of commodity production. The organic potatoes, in particular, show masterly branding and packaging, and consistent and delicious cooking results. (33 Mahon Road ☎ 028-9042 1883 www.wilsonscountry.com)

Delicatessen
● The Yellow Door Deli & Patisserie

Simon Dougan's cooking and baking is robust and tasty, and he has an instinct for succulence in his food that is truly pleasing. There is no conceit about his work: flavour and savour are the names of the game, flavour and savour are what he aims to produce every time, and flavour and savour are what you get. The daytime cooking at the Yellow Door is splendid: imaginative breakfasts such as warm blueberry pancakes with maple syrup or hot bacon and egg ciabatta; delicious lunches such as stuffed pork and green apple chutney sandwich complement yummy main dishes such as seafood parcels with white wine and dill sauce. The food-to-go would persuade you to hang up your own apron: superb venison pies; fish parcels; duck confit; rare roast beef; and a fab selection of salads are congratulated by choice bottles and their own chutneys and jams. A one-stop shop for food lovers. (74 Woodhouse St, Portadown
☎ 028-3835 3528, www.yellowdoordeli.com)

Tandragee

Bakery
● California Market Bakery

Unfortunately for northerners, Vince – the muffin man – McClean, and his wife Kathy – the baker – spend most of their retail time at markets in Dublin and beyond. However, you can go directly to the bakery, where their shop counter provides an aroma-filled insight to the secrets of their California cookery, especially if Vince is zesting lemons for the poppy seed muffins, or Kathy is opening the oven for the latest batch of cheese and bacon scones. They go to some lengths to source good fruits and the results of their efforts shine through in their super-sized oatmeal raspberry, pear pecan, and orange date creations – embodied by muffins, scones and cookies. (19 Church Street, Tandragee
☎ 028-3884 1616)

A grand day out...

· *Ballydougan Pottery* Snap up a tea pot, then sit down and snap up a pot of tea in these tea rooms attached to the popular pottery.

· *Great Hall at Queens* Gawp at the architectural splendour of this magnificent hall, while gulping down a very civilised self-service lunch of healthy, homely lunches, in the company of the academic staff from the university.

· *Linenhall Library* - Have a hushed cup of tea and regular scones and sandwiches aboved the muted roar of buses and general hustle and bustle in Donegall Square.

· *Dublin Road Movie House* - Always reliable for a thin 'n' crispy pizza with uncomplicated toppings and pure flavours, *Pizza Express* is the cinema canteen, and a great children's venue.

· *Seaforde Butterfly Farm* – Exceedingly good cakes are what will set your heart aflutter after or instead of a visit to the farm.

· *St George's* – Trevor's sodas, Flour's crêpes, and the Javaman's coffee and the big band sounds of St George's market will transform you from bleary-eyed to bushy tailed.

· *Donaghadee garden centre* – An ace garden centre now also has a new, improved coffee shop with lots of comforting lunches and gardeners' teabreak snacks. Also in Bushmills.

· *Slieve Gullion* – Serious 7-course dining once you've worked up an appetite on the mountainside.

· *Mountstewart Gardens* – A smart, well-run self-service café offering daily specials including Caesar salads, ham and egg quiches and shepherd's pies.

Annalong

Fish and Chip Shop

● Galley Fish and Chip Shop

The Galley's chips are the bee's knees. Made on
our most recent summer visit with new potatoes from Ballynahinch, and fried in dripping for
a melting crisp exterior and creamy interior, to
accompany fresh local battered cod, whiting or hake - in a
crunchy dry batter - they are also more than good enough
to eat on their own. A picnic bench of hanging baskets and
even decking is provided beside the tickety-boo shop, but
people still seem to prefer eating food from the Galley in
their cars. Perhaps they enjoy the lingering vinegary aroma
as much as we do. (43 Kilkeel Rd, Annalong ☎ 028-
4376 7253 – Open day time & dinner)

only in ulster

ardglass potted herring

Not to be confused with roll mops, this dish was created,
fishermen joke, to provide variety in the days when herring were so plentiful that they were boiled for starter,
fried for mains and potted for dessert. Each family has its
own secret variation, but often they are wrapped around
onion, bay leaf and all-spice with a 50:50 mixture of malt
vinegar and water, topped with breadcrumbs and baked.
We spotted them at the Ardglass convenience store's
checkout, but you'll also find them at markets, and in
traditional butchers throughout County Down.

Ardglass

Restaurant & Bar

● Currans Seafood & Steak Restaurant

Originally built in 1791, Currans' kitchen and parlours have
been turned into a cosy conglomeration of fire-lit bars, and

a formal restaurant. The ambitiously lengthy menu serves typical pub fare from battered chicken strips to Thai prawn curry. However, fresh seafood from Ardglass and dry hung steaks are the specialities here, and you will eat a good chowder lunch, fish and chip tea, or retro steak supper. (83 Strangford Road, Chapeltown, Ardglass ☎ 028-4484 1332 www.curransbar.net – Open lunch & dinner)

Fish Van
● **S&P Milligan**
Look out for the Milligan's fish van, whose fine selection of fresh fish from Ardglass attracts a healthy queue wherever it lands. Tuesday is Lisburn, Wednesday is Counties Antrim & Tyrone, Thursday is Ballynahinch, Friday is Cookstown and Belfast market, Saturday is Ballymena, and then they rest. (☎ 028-4484 1595)

Ballynahinch

Fish and Chip Café
● **Ginesi's**
Ginesi's famous fish and chip café is always full of people who turn up here time and again just as much for the charm of Gillian and Romano Ginesi as for their super fried fish and the cracklingly good Ulster fries. Ginesi's is a great stop-over if you have been building up an appetite hiking in the Mournes, so order up those good chips and a big stainless steel pot of tea and send that appetite packing. (34 Main St, Ballynahinch ☎ 028-9756 2653 – Open lunch & dinner)

Ballyward

Smokehouse
● **Drumgooland Smokehouse**
If ever there was a model family, it is the Smiths of Drumgooland Smoke House. While most parents of three teenage-plus children face hormone-induced strops and black-clad rebellion, the Smiths are harmoniously getting on with the business of

making good food. They make mostly hot smoked food with local ingredients, if they can get their hands on them. However, if you are comparing them to other artisans using traditional kilns, it is Suzanne's marinades and the variety of fruit woods and peat used for burning that makes her food different. Soaked in a recipe usually involving herbs, such as bay, Muscovado sugar and sometimes whiskey or Guinness (draught, to create a more subtle flavour than stout), legs of duck, breasts of chicken, whole trout or mackerel and pieces of Glenarm organic salmon, are air-dried and then hot smoked over cherry, pear, applewood, or peat. The result: gently smoky, subtly flavoured and rather succulent meats that need minimal dressing. Try their smoked duck, Suzanne says, with fresh pink grapefruit or Drumgooland orange chutney; their chicken sliced in a salad with a drizzle of good olive oil; and the salmon crumbled over pasta with fresh basil and crème fraîche. If you find them in the St George's market, don't miss out on husband Terence's terrific griddle breads or daughter Ciara's drinkable dressings. (4 Gargarry Road, Ballyward, nr Banbridge ☎ 028-4065 0720 www.drumgoolandsmokehouse.co.uk)

Bangor

Fish and Chips
● Bangor Fish Company

So, here's what to do if you have to feed a tribe of kids – such as the McKennas and their many Bangor cousins. First jump into the car, head down to the BFC, and order up a mountain of chips, some fresh cod and some smoked cod, and a welter of sausages and pasties. Then, submit it to the ultimate critical focus group: youngsters between the ages of 6 and twelve. How did the BFC do?

Very well, actually. Very well indeed. The chips were scoffed, the David Burns' sausages, likewise, but the real hit, surprisingly, was the smoked cod. You would imagine the younger chip connoisseur might be sceptical of smoked fish, but they all loved the saline-salty-smoky cod.

Harmony reigned around the table; parents even got a morsel or two, and the BFC done good. (20 High Street, Bangor ☎ 028-9147 2172 – Open day time & dinner)

Delicatessan and Café
● **Cafe Spice**

Kerry O'Brien has added in a few tables to the cosy Café
Spice, a great boon for those who want coffee and a cake
or a decent sandwich, albeit that it can make some of the
shelves a little more inaccessible, for Spice isn't a great big
emporium. But, what is crammed into Spice is always good,
and indeed there are many truly exceptional artisan foods
sold here, by a chirpy, lively crew who enjoy their work, and
who enjoy helping you to get exactly what you want. The
selection of Irish and European cheeses is always excellent,
and always in tip-top condition, so Spice is first stop for
Durrus farmhouse cheese or Parmigiano Reggiano, whilst
the olives and cured meats and other treats make home
entertaining a doddle. (7-9 Market Street ☎ 028-9147 7666
– Open day time)

only in ulster

traditional butcher's sausages

The fine-textured sausage typical in Northern Ireland is
very distinct from continental styles, and each butcher
has his own unique family recipe, usually made with natural casings and hand-linked. Beef sausages seem pecu-
liar to the north in Ireland, although they are also found in
Scotland.

Gastropub
● **Coyle's**

Mark Coyle's bar and upstairs restaurant has had a revamp,
but the central tenet of Ian Morrow's cooking in this lively
gastropub remains rock-solid: imaginative modern food that
roams around international flavours from polenta to
Portavogie prawn butter, whilst still able to deliver a very
succulent County Down beef burger and properly cooked
seafood for more cautious consumers. Food and wines are
chosen with considerable care, and whilst service can be
stretched too much at busy times, this is a gastropub with
huge potential and no little ambition. The daytime bar food

is simpler than the restaurant offering, but food lovers
should wait for the evening and head upstairs to see just
what Mr Morrow can do. It's delightful, also to see the
Bangor tradition of quirky, unexpected eating places – anyone remember The Back Street Café, or Genoa Bistro? –
continuing in its quirky, unexpected fashion. (44 High Street,
Bangor ☎ 028-91290362 – Open lunch (bar food) & dinner)

Butcher
● **David Burns Butchers**

Brian and George Burns innovate quietly in
their trim, super-busy butchers shop at the top
of Abbey Street. Superficially, the range seems
to be consistent, but from time to time there
will be surprises: a new bacon cure for some thick-cut
bacon, or a new presentation of an old favourite, or a brand
new meat pie. This steady, conservative creativity means
that Burns keeps everyone happy, from the folk who want
the same-old same-old to the ambitious cooks who want
the strange stuff, the off-cuts, the offal and the extremities.
Service is always cheerful and resoundingly efficient, from
the Xmas turkey – again, quite wonderful – to their pork
sausages. And, indeed, regarding those pork sausages, we
have to enter a special commendation, for they seem to us
to be pretty much the most perfect banger you can buy,
and their consistent excellence is an perfect example of the
stellar standards this exemplary shop delivers day-in, day-
out. (112 Abbey Street, Bangor ☎ 028-9127 0073)

Home Bakery
● **Heatherlea**

"I would like to make myself windswept and interesting"
says Andrew Getty, who runs the Heatherlea with his
brother Paul, "but we can't sell things like rock salt bread.
We've had some success with our onion bread but basically
we make good quality, wholesome, traditional food." That
includes the 1000-odd scones they shift on market days and
Saturdays, and people travel from all over Northern Ireland
for the Heatherlea's wheaten, a fine-textured, moist bread,
with good cutting quality. Wheaten rounds, fruit loaves and
"sides" - two farls joined in the middle to create a semi-
circle - and the Belfast Baps also sell like hot cakes from the
shelves of this Bangor bakery. (4 Main Street, Bangor ☎ 028-
9145 3157 – Open day time)

Fishmonger
● McKeown's Fish Shop

McKeown's may look straightforward, but there
is ambition and creativity to be found in this
singular fishmongers. The standard wet fish is
always superb quality – indeed, it is one of the
benchmarks that show how bad supermarket fish counters
actually are – but it is when the team at McKeown's get
down to their own smoking and prepping and cooking of
their fish that you can see the energy and striving for excellence that animates this super shop. The people of Bangor
are fortunate indeed to have such excellent culinary crafts-
manship taking care of all their piscine needs. (14 High
Street, Bangor ☎ 028-9127 1141)

Preserves
● The Offbeat Bottling Company

"When it came down to the final judging, The
Offbeat Bottling Company's Extremely Orange
Marmalade was neck and neck with a blackcurrant jam for the Supreme Champion title," said
Bob Farrand of the Fine Food Retailers. "There was less
than one point between them, but the marmalade was just
pipped at the post… this was the closest contest we have
ever seen in the history of the awards…." Nail biting stuff,
at the Great Taste Awards, but Offbeat do produce finger-
licking preserves, chutneys and flavoured oils. I'll have a jar
of gin and bitter lemon please. And then an orange liqueur.
Who cares if they weren't best in show? (Unit 73
Enterprise House, 2/4 Balloo Avenue, Bangor
☎ 028-9127 1525)

Banbridge

Butcher
● MA Quail

"Purveyors of fine foods" is how Jim Quail
describes his excellent butcher's shop and delicatessen. And whilst it is certainly true that
Quail's purveys fine foods, what is of perhaps
even greater importance is the fact that Quail's sources and
selects fine foods to begin with, and does so with unerring

care. The names of the farms and farmers from whom Quail's meat is sourced locally is proudly displayed, but this vital, meaningful, humane, welfare-based traceability is something Jim Quail has always vividly demonstrated, even before it was made mandatory. It shows the partnership of trust between farmer and butcher/retailer that is the secret of successful shopping and cooking. Getting that success on the plate is what Jim Quail promises, but rather than creating an empty promise through advertising and public relations, Quail's delivers the real promise of success thanks to understanding the culture of charcuterie, and of good food. (13-15 Newry Street, Banbridge ☎ 028-4066 2604)

Home Bakery
● Windsor Bakery

Gordon Scott's smashing bakery is one of the pivotal addresses in Banbridge, a beacon of good baking and great service that seems to manage to shine brighter and brighter as the years go by. All the favourite Northern Ireland speciality breads are baked and sold here, the fadges and farls, the baps and apple sodas, the Coconut Shuttle and the Iced Finger – there is a book to be written about the names of Northern Irish patisserie and breads – and the Windsor is particularly noteworthy for having mastery of both sweet and savoury foods. In fact, you can buy anything in Mr Scott's shop – from a bumper birthday cake to a sausage roll to take-away – secure in the knowledge that confident expertise has originated, shaped and proved, baked and sold the final delicious product. (36-38 Newry Street, Banbridge ☎ 028-4062 3666)

Comber

Restaurant & Café
● The Georgian House

Ian Shannon's Georgian House is one of the first completed examples of the redevelopment of Comber's pretty and imposing village-centre square. It has already been colonised by locals of all ages as a favourite lunchtime spot for dishes such as potato and watercress soup, or their generous helping of breads with various dips, or specials such as salmon fish cakes, and the locals follow up lunch with a spot of

browsing and buying in the shop upstairs, which has homeware and also some canvases by Northern Irish painters. At
present, they open for dinner at weekend nights, and stage
two of the development should see the introduction of a
beer garden and a dedicated gallery space. A lovely spot to
take your Mum if you are out for a jaunt and some lunch,
interspersed with a little light shopping. (14 The Square,
Comber ☎ 028-9187 1818 – Open lunch & dinner)

only in ulster

the Irish moiled cow

A native of County Down, possibly introduced by Viking
settlers, these pretty white, flecked brown cattle with
brown ears and a brown muzzle were great "dual purpose" cows producing enough milk and rearing a calf for
enough meat to feed the smallhold farmer and his family.
By 1980 there were only 12 animals with pure Irish ances-
try, belonging to the Glenbrook and Maymore herds in
Ballymena and Killyleagh and it is still one of the rarest
bovine breeds. However, thanks to the work of the Irish
Moiled Cattle Society established in Glasdrumman in
1926, and the Rare Breeds Society there are now 120
breeding females locally, and the same again in the UK,
which trace their origins to Northern Ireland. It may seem
ironic that we have to eat these animals to ensure the
survival of the breed, but you can do your bit by becom-
ing a hobby farmer, or by popping into Pheasants Hill
Rare Breed Meat Shop in Comber for their marbled meat.

Farm Shop
● Pheasants Hill Farm Shop & Butcher's Shop
Alan and Janis Bailey's Pheasant's Hill shop is
one of the most important food shops in
Ireland, for two reasons. Firstly, Mr Bailey is
devoted to rare breed animals, so what you will
find here you will not find anywhere else.
Secondly, this man thinks like an epicurean; from the initial

product, this farmer-cum-shopkeeper and his team cansee, smell and taste the finished dish. "It's the breed, the feed, the matur-ity," says Mr Bailey, and the level of knowledge about the fresh meats sold here is superlative. Dexter beef, for instance, will have been reared on marginal land, will never have been fed concentrates, it will have been sourced through the Dexter Society, and will have been slaughtered nearby in Lurgan, creating all the ideal conditions for superb beef. Tamworth, saddleback and Gloucester old spot are the chosen pig breeds, and whilst Mr Bailey attests to the superb hams from Tamworth animals, don't on any account miss the glorious, sweet bacon the Tamworth gifts us with. Just as importantly, these magnificent pigs will have been reared to 45 weeks' maturity, more than twice the life cycle of the conventional pig. And, when he makes a sausage, Mr Bailey stresses that he is "trying to bring out the flavour of the meat", so the sausages here are utterly distinctive. Alongside the Dexter, there is also Irish Moiled beef, and some Angus, the Moiled being a milder flavour. For lamb, the meat will be almost 1 year old, either Oxford Down or Southdowns or Wensleydale, whilst mutton can be over four years' old, and will have been hung for a month. Mutton heaven! The store is also packed with great organic foods, from milk to smoked salmon, and Mr Bailey has already begun the quest for creating the perfect chicken for the table. Pheasant's Hill is an inspiration, and a unique, un-missable address. (3 Bridge Street Link, Comber ☎ 028-9187 8470)

Crossgar

Local Shop
● John Colgan's

Colgan's is a fine family shop to find in a small village like Crossgar, with a neat deli counter, and good local vegetables. (49a Downpatrick Street Crossgar ☎ 028-4483 1056)

Local Shop
● Fitzsimon's Newsagents

Alistair and Steven Fitzsimon's shop is a destination for creamy, traditional homemade vanilla ice-cream. (42 Downpatrick Road, Crossgar ☎ 028-4483 0032)

Wine Merchant
● James Nicholson Wine Merchants

Most folk with a quarter century or so of
being at the cutting edge of sourcing and
selling great wines from all over the world
might think it was time to kick back and
take it easy, and open up a bottle or two of
the Hecht & Bannier from Minervois or
the Zuani 2004 from the Collio hills.
Well, no one seems to have told Jim Nicholson
that he can take it easy. The 2005 list from
Nicholson's had no fewer than 130 new wines and, by
late 2006, Jim Nicholson will have a brand new shop and
warehouse a few doors down Killyleagh Street, a project he
has been nursing for much of the last decade, a period of
time when he has also been garnering awards galore for a
list that has an unerring instinct for great wines. We rather
feel that Nicholson's success is built on instinct, an instinct
for people, and an instinct for the wines these people make.
The interesting thing about the JN list is how concordant it
is; there are no brash or bullying wines here, just subtle,
interesting, cultured wines, made by subtle, cultured and
interesting people, howsoever different they may be (and
they are different: meet John Forrest from New Zealand,
and then meet Randall Grahm from California, and you
meet two polar opposites of the male psyche, not to mention the wine psyche). Jim and Elspeth Nicholson manage to
corrall these diverse folk and their diverse wines into a sin-
uously arranged and orchestrated wine list, and they sell
these wines from a groovy shop, and through an amazingly
efficient web site and delivery service. The day you walk
through that door on Killyleagh Street is one of those few
days when your life takes a turn for the better.
(Killyleagh St, Crossgar ☎ 028-4483 0091 www.jnwine.com)

Donaghadee

Garden Centre Café
● Donaghadee Garden Centre
Richard Gibson, of Smith & Gibson, masterminds the delicious food both here and in the Bushmills garden centre.
(34 Stockbridge Road, Donaghadee ☎ 028-9188 3603)

Ice Cream
● The Cabin

Pastel pale tongue and groove, old fashioned stainless steel freezers, and homemade vanilla ice-cream are available at this quaint and popular seaside destination. (32 New Street, Donaghadee ☎ 028-9188 3598)

Gastropub
● Pier 36

Raeburn-cooked roasts and breads, and simple seafood, sometimes brought direct from the pier in Donaghadee, are key attractions on the menu at Pier 36, a successful, service-focused, family-run pub, now moving towards its self-assured second generation. However, it's Denis and Margaret Waterworth who really should be credited for the charming, genuine welcome, the open fires, and the homely approach that makes this place a good high tea option. Menus can dip into overcomplicated dishes aping global trends, so Pier 36 is best for its local vernacular dishes, which suits the pub setting. Don't be scared off by the supreme of chicken on Gorgonzola ravioli with tiger prawn mousseline in vegetable saffron broth, because for every dish like this, there's a braised beef olives on shallot mash with carrot and parsnip purée and red wine jus, or Demerara-glazed gammon with Savoy cabbage, baby boiled potatoes and lashings of butter. (36 The Parade, Donaghadee ☎ 028-9188 4466, www.pier36.co.uk – Open lunch & dinner)

Downpatrick

B&B
● Ballymote House

If you're a food-lover looking for somewhere to stay in St Patrick's country, then there's nowhere nicer than Ballymote, a pretty Georgian B&B and well-worn family home, stuffed full of fine hand-me-down antiques, faded silk curtains and pure-bred dogs. Blissful beds, huge bathtubs, log and hand-cut turf fires await you and Nicola, an enthusiastic well practised cook, gives ingredients - from local butchers, the family estate, and the boats at Ardglass - a sophisticated Cordon Bleu treatment.

You need to allow plenty of advance warning if there's a large party, or if you'd like to experience the aristocratic charm of the dining room. However, even at short notice, Nicola will churn out delicious suppers – such as the legendary stone of langoustines and bottle of Chablis - while chattering away about horsey pursuits and all the other activities you can pursue in this monument, holy well and stone circle-littered countryside.

We enjoyed an earthy artichoke soup, followed by mains of a skilfully succulent pheasant - fried in goose fat and finished with Marsala, grapes and cream - before a decent farm house cheeseboard, strong coffee - and a great night's sleep. Breakfast changes daily for long-stay guests and is served from a help-yourself platter, around the big, friendly kitchen table. If it wasn't for the spectacular views of the Mournes sweeping down to the sea as you drive out of the front gates, leaving this place would be unbearable. (Killough Road, Downpatrick ☎ 028-4461 5500 www.ballymotehouse.com)

Gastropub
● Denvirs

One of the few places where you can get a bite to eat after dark in Downpatrick, this ancient pub and coaching house is good for conservative choices such as steak, salad and chips rather than anything more ambitious. It's tasty food with lashings of sauce, and garlic potatoes. (English Street, Downpatrick ☎ 028-4461 2012 – Open lunch & dinner)

Venison
● Finnebrogue Venison

Denis Lynn farms only red deer on the 600 acres of Finnebrogue, and slaughters before the animals are 18 months in order to obtain a milder, more tender meat. This is not the wild, chewy, gamey venison we associate with long-simmered stews, but a lighter, more consistent style of game that is raised as naturally as possible. Finnebrogue have created a range of venison sausages in collaboration with stellar chef Andy Rea, and hip packaging for their retail line should see this assured and ambitious endeavour winding up on more and more dinner plates. This is a dynamic enterprise that bodes well for farming and also our own health. (Finnebrogue Estate, Downpatrick ☎ 028-4461 7525 www.finnebrogue.com)

Local Shop
● Hanlon's

This sweet old-style general store has shelves groaning and aisles cluttered with a little bit of everything – a fish counter with fresh fish, local vegetables, Irish cheeses, groceries, wholefoods and some good-quality baking ingredients – and the nifty male staff dressed in their blue overalls and grocers' hats are just the ticket. (26 Market Street, Downpatrick ☎ 028 4461 2518)

Farm Shop & Guesthouse
● Pheasant's Hill Farm Shop & Guesthouse

See the entry for the Pheasants Hill shop in Comber for background on the rare breeds that Janis and Alan Bailey specialise in. You can also buy frozen meat from the house, and there is a comfortable and welcoming B&B with pretty rooms for those who wish to languorously loiter amidst the calm beauty of South Down. (37 Killyleagh Road, Downpatrick ☎ 028-4461 7246)

Dundrum

Restaurant
● The Buck's Head

Dramatic high ceilings, bog oak sculptures, velvet striped and spotted scatter cushions, and walls of silky cherry wood, are just part of the reason for the rolling boil atmosphere at the Buck's Head. Alison Carruthers also knocks out stonking 'pub' lunches of fishcakes and savoury tarts, high teas of battered scampi and chips, before slowing the pace, and taking the food up a gear for the simple fusion of traditional and modern cuisine found in her set dinner menu. Sea-fresh, meaty tempura oysters come in craggy shells with a chilli, soy and sesame oil dip. Melon balls bob in an exotic fruit soup. Crunchy vegetable tagliatelle and a delicious citrus butter make for a memorable monkfish while succulent chicken is paired with a delicate fennel purée and basil oil. You can't diverge from a three-course menu, but giant berry strewn meringues, and warm slabs of brownie with a trail of thickened cream make that an effortless challenge. (77 Main Street, Dundrum ☎ 028-4375 1868 – Open lunch & dinner)

Guesthouse
● The Carriage House

Bright and uncluttered, Maureen Griffith's interiors sympathetically juxtapose delicate
antiques with authentic retro and modern furnishings, and display a personal and eclectic
selection of art. Her three bedrooms are homely and indul-
gent, with tasteful, treat-filled trays, powerful showers, fresh
flowers, finely perfumed soaps, and plump beds piled high
with soft pillows in fine cotton. Breakfasts are also a delight,
with just made fruit salads, star-anise spiced plums, herby
butcher's sausages, and local or homemade breads. Her
sun-exposed garden, with fabulous horse sculpture, has
lovely views over Dundrum Bay and provides a playground
for pet labradors, hedgehogs, and grandchildren in this most
relaxing home from home. (71 Main Street, Dundrum
☎ 028-4375 1635 www.carriagehousedundrum.com)

Oyster Fishery
● Dundrum Bay Oyster Fishery

Dundrum are suppliers of carefully cultivated shellfish to
the restaurant trade. You can try before you buy at the fishery's loyal local customer, the Buck's Head. The meaty
Pacific oysters are very versatile, good eaten raw with just
lemon juice and Tabasco, or grilled with a strong cheddar.
DBOF also grow mussels and cockles, and advise packing
them in parcels with herbs and spices for the barbecue
when you've had enough of moules mariniere or spaghetti
alle vongole. (☎ 028-4375 1810, www.dundrumbayoysters.co.uk)

Seafood Bar
● Mourne Seafood Bar

If it weren't for the off-putting time limits allocated to diners, there would be little hesitation in recommending this
newcomer to Dundrum. Well-worn floorboards, salvaged,
wooden furniture, assorted sea-themed art by talented
locals is the perfect casual setting in a grand old building for
a roll-your-sleeves up, finger-licking menu of grilled, shell-on
langoustines, kilo-pots of mussels, Carlingford oysters, and
hot and cold seafood platters. A full blackboard of daily specials sometimes puts a little too much pressure on the
kitchen, and the fish is not always in tip-top condition.
However, for every disappointment – a wet linguini dish
with mussels, and white wine cream, or grey, lifeless sole -

there is a dazzling hit, such as the glistening fresh hake with avocado salsa or the meaty ling, with red wine cream. Stunning display is another forte of the food, and when the operational kinks are ironed out, the Mourne could and should advance towards major status. (10 Main St, Dundrum ☎ 028-4375 1377 – Open lunch & dinner)

Gilford

Restaurant
● **Mill Street**

With a welcome of revolving glitter balls, sparkling chandeliers, and dazzling smiles, you know you're in for a night of fun at Mill Street. Dinner starts with cocktails and martini glasses of Bombay mix in the tea-lit, silk-lined lounge bar. And once you've chosen from the luxury-studded menu, where the New World meets Northern Ireland (chef's pâté with redcurrant and port compote, "black and white" steak – with bearnaise), you're taken upstairs for some more gobsmacking interiors, and some gobsmacking food. Battered Pacific oysters come with a shell-lickingly good lime-laced raw tomato salsa, a rosemary-infused chicken terrine is layered with fine green beans and works well with a fresh plum and ginger syrup, a fat-crisp leg of lamb has a spiky hit of marinated sweet onion, and a soft cushion of fleshy sweet butternut squash. Lack of manpower is the excuse for disappointing bought-in desserts, but a big front of house personality softens the blow. (14 Mill Street, Gilford ☎ 028-3883 1166 – Open lunch & dinner)

Restaurant
● **The Oriel**

The people of Gilford and further afield will miss Barry Smyth, who has decided to take a short sabbatical from the business and consider new options before he re-emerges back into the restaurant world. Mr Smyth will be missed by a devoted local audience who respected the fact that even though this gifted cook had won stellar awards for his work in The Oriel, he remained a chef who looked after his local audience first. That is no small matter, for the world of cookery is filled with chefs who quickly forget their roots, and their cooking always suffers as a result.

But Mr Smyth's audience was greater than just happy locals, and it is no exaggeration to say that The Oriel was one of the best-loved restaurants in Northern Ireland. His fans, therefore, will wait anxiously for him to reappear, and they will be able to find out what he will be doing from his website, www.orielrestaurant.com, an address to which you can also send Mr Smyth an email to find out what's cooking.

only in ulster

pasties

"Proper kids' food" is how butcher George Burns describes Ulster's pasties (note: the singular of this noun is "pastie"). This comforting mixture of sausage meat, onions and mashed potato is shaped like a burger, and always spiced with loads and loads and loads of black pepper. You can order them plain, battered – the chip shop favourite – or coated with golden breadcrumbs. Or grown-ups can have the chi chi version where the pastie is coated in a crushed pepper crust.

Greyabbey

Butcher
● Angus Farm Shop

Meat is cut to order for customers in this tiny village butchers, which sells the produce from grass-fed animals from the family farm, as well as local eggs, a sensible selection of useful vegetables, and a few well-chosen condiments and marinades. Regulars can make special orders for produce not generally available, and you may need to reserve prime cuts in advance, as Noel will not sell any meat that is not properly matured and ready for the oven, a sound practice that guarantees a fairly constant queue of people in the shop who leave weighed down by heavy bags in each hand filled with good things. (42 Main Street, Greyabbey
☎ 028-4278 8695)

Craft Shop & Café
● Pebbles

Rachel and Ron's pretty wee craft shop and cafe has a day-time savoury menu that veers from humongous mixed grills of steak, chicken, sausage and bacon, or burgers with 'wedges' and dips, all the way to wild mushroom risotto with rocket. A rather good shellfish-packed chowder bodes well for the monthly Friday night bistro when the chef tries his hand at an appealing three-course menu of, say, warm parsley salad with haricot beans and tongue, baked hake with courgettes, lemon and thyme, and brown sugar meringues with sugared figs. Decent espresso coffees are also served. (12 Main Street, Greyabbey ☎ 028-4278 8031 – Open day time)

Coffee Shop
● Hoops Coffee Shop

Decked out with antique pine, Van Gogh chairs and blue gingham, Sandra Kelso's Hoops is a homely kind of place run by capable mature ladies assisted by not-so-capable school kids. The coffee isn't hectic, but then this is the place for a good cup of tea, and excellent home-baked cakes – try the orange drizzle or coffee and walnut. Lunches, such as the gratifying smoked salmon quiche, leek and potato pie or baked ham salad are simple, generous and tasty. (7 Main Street, Greyabbey ☎ 028-4278 8091 – Open day time)

Groomsport

Wine Merchant
● Classic Wine

Robert Neill's wine shop is a wee beauty, powered by the energy and wine-loving pizazz of the man himself. This man loves the business of wines, he loves the passionate work of winemakers, he loves the thrill presented by simply uncork-ing, unscrewing and pouring each bottle, and it shows. His newsletters, for example, are a pure blast of irreverence: wines from Domaine Michel Fonne are "mind blowing in terms of their intrinsic quality, authenticity, purity", whilst it is "mind boggling as to why this fairy-tale wine region is always overlooked by consumers". Mind blowing and mind boggling in one sentence: Mr Neill should be writing for the Bridgestone guides! You can see this energy and joie de vin in action at the many tastings and dinners Mr Neill creates, and for a regular blast of it you can join their Cellar Door club, where a case of new arrivals and favourites will be dispatched on a monthly or bi-monthly basis. Like certain other elements of the food culture in Northern Ireland – butchers' shops, homeware stores, home bakeries – standards amongst wine sellers are stratospheric, and Classic Wine fits comfortably into that stellar groove. (49 Main St, Groomsport ☎ 028-9147 8982)

Helen's Bay

Organic Farm
● **Helen's Bay Organic Farm**
If you live in the North Down zone and you are not the recipient of one of John McCormick's weekly delivery boxes of produce from his farm at Helen's Bay, then your life isn't as good as it could be. For Mr McCormick isn't simply one of the pioneer organic growers, he is one of the finest organic growers, his vegetables demonstrating and revealing the careful, patient and philosophical compass of a gifted agriculturist. If you are foolish enough to retain any doubts about the superiority of organic produce over chemically-produced agriculture, then a box of fresh vegetables from Mr McCormick will show you exactly what organoleptic possibilities can be achieved by a great grower working in harmony with nature. Cooking with these vegetables is a pure joy and delight. (Coastguard Avenue, Helen's Bay ☎ 028-9185 3122)

Hillsborough

Café Bar
● **Barretro**
Barretro is run by the same team who oversee the popular Plough Bistro right next door. The concept offers casual cooking, cocktails and cool sounds. (Coastguard Avenue, Hillsborough ☎ 028-9268 2985 www.barretro.com – Open daytime & early evening at weekends)

Bistro
● The Plough Bistro

Derek Patterson's popular PB has a traditional pub ambience, thanks to low ceilings, padded nooks for seating and white-washed walls, the right sort of cosy setting for a bustlingly busy pub that packs in the punters for generous helpings of food that pull together influences from all over the globe. The staff are well up to keeping up with the demands of the crowds, and indeed turning up to The Plough with a bunch of your best mates is the best way to get the best out of this Hillsborough landmark. (The Square, Hillsborough ☎ 028-9268 2985 www.barretro.com)

Hilltown

Chipper
● The Hilltown Chippy

Paul Smith has a quarter century of expert judicious fish frying and chip production under his belt. The Hilltown is more than worth a detour and we recommend you bring along a bunch of your friends and then pose the eternal question: are these the best chips in the Western World? And, if so, does that make Hilltown Chip Central, Planet Earth? (Main Street, Hilltown ☎ 028-4063 8130)

Holywood

Café
● The Bay Tree

Is there anything better, at 9.30am, than a Bay Tree cinnamon scone and a cup of tea or coffee? We don't think so. It's so great that one can let the babble of Holywood mums discussing due dates, epidurals and induced births float right over your head, as the scent of fine baking and the toasty coffee takes you right to Blissville. That's the sort of thing Sue Farmer and her team achieve in The Bay Tree: food that transports you out of yourself, whether you are simply having a bowl of chunky vegetable soup or a salad of Puy lentils with goat's cheese and walnuts, or whether you are one of the lucky people who have managed a reservation for the Friday night's dinner, and you are suddenly looking forward to lemongrass and coriander vichyssoise, followed by cous cous crusted aubergine with almond, chilli and scallion stuffing and a sweet pepper concassé, and then a raspberry crusted brûlée with mascarpone to finish dinner on a rousing sweet note. Ms Farmer is one of the great cooks, a person whose food bristles with freshness, creativity and ingenuity, a cook who can stamp her signature on a classic lamb biryani as effortlessly as she will sign off a dish or panzanella or poached haddock with mussels, spinach and chervil. Great cooking. (118 High Street, Holywood ☎ 028-9042 1419 – Open day time & dinner on Fri)

Café
● Café Kina

Opened by Karen Ferguson, a former team-member from Cargoes on Belfast's Lisburn Road, and Niko Thomas, her French patissier husband, Café Kina follows the Cargoes formula with domestic goddess cakes, Gallic pastries, deli sandwiches, and a discerning home-catering menu. However there is a more conventional approach with its specials menu, when sizzling satay skewers, pork and apple burgers, steak sandwiches and bubbling veggie bakes are served with sides of wedges or potato salad. (81 High Street, Holywood ☎ 028-9042 5216 – Open day time)

Organic Shop & Bakery
● Camphill Organic Farm Shop & Bakery

Rob van Duin's fantastic breads are frequently cited by regulars as the main attraction at the calm and elemental Camphill shop and café, but you shouldn't overlook the organic fruit and veg, and the tasty food in the café, for this trilogy of attractions adds up to one of the best food shops in Northern Ireland. You can source Organic Doorstep milk, Oakdene Organics cream (and very good it is too), Arkhill farm eggs from Garvagh, amidst a plethora of wholefoods. But, the breads are indeed special, and Mr van Duin's skill means that they are not merely wholesome: they are also precise and pleasing. (Shore Road, Holywood ☎ 028-9042 3203)

Kitchenshop
● La Cucina

Tightly packed with good things of every size and shape for the kitchen, Cucina is a cracking shop. It is one of those places that manages to have just what you want and need, whether it's a turbo-charged caffeine machine for making espressos or just a really good working cook's knife. It's all good value too; you'll see things here that are quite a lot cheaper than in other city centre stores. Cucina is a key part of the hip, hot Holywood hub of eating and shopping. (63 High Street, Holywood ☎ 028-9042 2118)

Restaurant
● Fontana

Fontana is one of those restaurants that seems to get better and better, by steady, accumulative, aggregate steps. Right now, the kitchen in Colleen Bennet's restaurant is firing out some mighty food, and it is served to happy punters in a sweet dining room by really excellent staff who look after you extra well. Oh, and they offer great value, and super wines. Could you want for more? No, you couldn't. Ms Bennet has always made a rip-roaring risotto – we recall her knocking an audience for six back at the St George's Market in 1999 when she made a risotto with mussels and crab meat – and the current offering of prawn risotto with sweetcorn, courgettes, peas, chilli and coriander is one of the most subtle things you can eat, the flavours lifted by a suggestion of coconut, the whole dish a blessed thing altogether – and also one of the highlight dishes of 2005. But there's more: superb potato and truffle oil soup; fab Drumgooland smoked salmon with blue Roosevelt potatoes, green beans, olives and egg; really fine grilled rainbow trout, and a knockout chocolate mousse with fresh raspberries that the McKenna children ate so swiftly that there wasn't a morsel left for the grown ups to try. Mighty food and mighty fun, Fontana is on a mighty roll. (61a High St Holywood ☎ 028-9080 9908 www.fontanarestaurant.com)

Wholefood Shop & Bistro
● The Iona

The long-established Iona has morphed into an alternatives shop more than a food stop in recent times, though you

can still find herbs and some wholefoods for sale here. The
Iona Bistro upstairs offers some simple food and its survival
is testimony to an enduring care and application. (27
Church Road, Holywood ☎ 028-9042 8597. Bistro Iona
☎ 028-9042 5655)

Butcher & Deli
● **Orr's**

Butchery, deli, and wet fish store all rolled into one, this is
the place to buy well matured meat, free-range chickens,
sausages made with natural casings, their own cooked ham,
Sprott's dry cure bacon, eggs from Whinney Hill, Gerry's
own recipe potted herrings, Manx kippers, wild salmon and
seatrout in season, naturally smoked haddock, Gerry's sister's homemade pavlova bases, and SD Bell's teas and coffees, to name but a few items. With lino floors, warping
shelves and charming service, Orrs is the equivalent of a
rural Italian food store, so there's no surprise they have sur-
vived the arrival of the supermarket giants down the road.
(56 High Street, Holywood ☎ 028-9042 2288)

only in ulster

hardnuts

**Crunchy sweets rather than tough lads, these are the off-
cuts from ginger biscuits, which were traditionally sold at
country fairs.**

Restaurant
● **Sullivan's**

Simon Shaw hits all the spots at the amiable Sullivan's, one
of the quintessential neighbourhood restaurants, Indeed, it's
such a neighbourly place that the customers in here seem
almost to treat it as if it was their own home: a space for
coffee at 11, a space for lunch or brunch at noon, a place
for a friendly dinner at 8pm. That is what a local restaurant
should achieve, and that is exactly what Mr Shaw and his
crew achieve. Part of his secret lies in offering not just
good, tasty modern food - panini of goat's cheese with
olives and roasted vegetables; Mediterranean tomato soup;
good pasta dishes; nice roast meats for dinner – but in also

offering excellent value for money. Modest, efficient and hard-working, there could and should be a Sullivan's in every town in Northern Ireland. After all, where else can you get an Ulster Fry, with a glass of champagne? Now that's the way to start the day. (2 Sullivan Place, Holywood ☎ 028-9042 1000 www.sullivansrestaurant.co.uk – Open lunch & dinner)

Kilkeel

Brewery
● The Whitewater Brewing Company

The Whitewater is one of only two craft brewers in Northern Ireland, along with the long-established Hilden. They produce a dozen cask-conditioned ales and a lager, and you will find them for sale in good pubs throughout the province. (40 Tullyframe Road, Kilkeel ☎ 028-4176 9449 www.whitewaterbrewing.co.uk)

Killyleagh

Gastropub
● Dufferin Arms

The Dufferin has been serving beers since 1803, and is now one of the best places for a pint of the black stuff. People also travel from afar for a bowl of the Dufferin Arms' chowder, and traditional folk and blue grass sessions, when musicians may outnumber customers in the snugs upstairs. Or you can eat quite well in its basement restaurant, where an impressive effort is made to source local ingredients, such as Finnebrogue venison, summertime seafood from the lough, and specials such as Guinness and oysters or pheasant casserole with chestnuts and mushrooms are served. (35 High St, Killyleagh, ☎ 028 4482 1182, www.dufferinarms.com – Open lunch & dinner)

Delicatessen
● Picnic

"I came here for a pint and stayed" says deli-owner John Dougherty of his adoptive hometown, Killyleagh. Now he and his Australian wife, and her backpacker cousins run an excellent and very dinky 6' square deli-café whose generously packed shelves, sturdy baskets, and tiered cake stands lure customers with an irresistible and discerning choice of cheese, charcuterie, cakes, sweetmeats and deli goodies. A typical lunch might be herby drop scones, served with mascarpone, roast red pepper, and heaps of deliciously dressed salad, followed by flourless chocolate cake, a toasty espresso, and a chunk or two of that pistachio-studded, icing sugar dusted Turkish delight. No wonder that crowd of cyclists stop here every Sunday for breakfast. (49 High Street, Killyleagh ☎ 028 4482 8525 – Open day time)

Ceramics
● Viva Ceramica

The outlet for bold, brightly painted handmade Italian pottery - from teeny-weeny espresso cups to huge great lemonade pitchers - and stunning Picasso-inspired urns, candlesticks and platters by Susannah Desimone. (6 High Street, Killyleagh ☎ 028 4482 8392, www.vivaceramica.com)

Kircubbin

Restaurant
● Paul Arthurs

Foie gras, lobster, venison and partridge are seasonal staples at Paul Arthur's, but this doesn't mean you have to dress up to come and eat here. For anything goes at this bright, laid-back brasserie, run by a fiercely independent one-man band in the kitchen, and a few bright young waitresses. Come here after a day on the lough, although people will travel miles just to eat Arthurs' chunky smoked haddock chowder, with its milky chive-flecked liquor, his cracked crab claws dripping with a hot butter of lemon, garlic and chilli, his billowy gnocchi with Gorgonzola cream. Then comes a whack of sirloin, all the better for Arthurs' butchery background, char-grilled and oozing with a spiced Café de Paris butter, pink honey-roast duck with shiitake, thick soy and sake, or some amazing catch of the day – turbot, Strangford prawns, Dover sole – all treated with the same flavour-focused flair. Desserts are dead simple and deadly. And you can crash for the night in their new rooms. You may well need to. (66 Main Street, Kircubbin ☎ 028-4273 8192 – Open dinner & Sun lunch)

Accommodation
● Paul Arthurs Rooms

Paul Arthurs has introduced the dynamic concept of the Restaurant with Rooms to Northern Ireland, adding on seven bedrooms to his restaurant – and chip shop – in the centre of Kircubbin. It's a smart move: Mr Arthurs food is worth travelling for, and being able to make a night of it down the peninsula with comfortable, inexpensive rooms is good news.

The rooms have oodles of character, thanks to the use of exposed brick and moody paintings, and the bathrooms are full-scale wet rooms with dark slate floors and powerful showers. The doors are at present a little bit creaky and hard to manage, and consequently create quite a lot of noise. But the linens are good, the towels are good – though toiletries should be provided – and breakfast, whilst somewhat predictable, is well-executed in the bright dining room. Everything about Paul Arthurs' rooms reveals the care and attention to detail of a good crew, and PA shouldn't be missed. (66 Main Street, Kircubbin ☎ 028 4273 8192)

Lisbane

B&B
● Anna's House

Anna and Ken Johnson's house is the ultimate cult destination in Northern Ireland. A gorgeous house, a gorgeous garden, gorgeous cooking, Anna's is the sort of house that man- ages to evoke the most elemental feelings about hospitality, food and our place in the world. Anna's is 14 miles from Belfast, but feels a zillion miles from the real world. Step in here and you step into a dream, or at least into some imagined world from your childhood, a space where you are woken by the smells of morning baking, a space where you can lose yourself in an afternoon in the garden, where you can chat away to people you have just met and yet feel you have known them all your life. Does that sound like hyperbole? Well check this script from a pair of German visitors: "This is the ideal B&B... great cooking, comfy rooms and superb hospitality. Anna and Ken you're great.. it felt like coming home". Feels like coming home, indeed. (Tullynagee, 35 Lisbarnett Road, Comber ☎ 028-9754 1566 www.annashouse.com)

Café & Craft Shop
● The Old Post Office Café

A partially thatched warren of tea and craft rooms with stoves and open fires burning peat, the Old Post Office is a cosy spot for the winter months, while picnic benches and a cottage garden provide a pleasant fair-weather setting. Cakes and desserts have a uniform appearance, but actually all food is made fresh daily by the owners, Trevor & Alison Smylie, who are also the village bakers. You can enjoy homely lunches of, say, lasagne and salad from a selection in neat bowls, or Irish Stew. (191 Killinchy Road, Lisbane, Comber ☎ 028-9754 3335 – Open day time)

Millisle

Pottery
● Eden Pottery

When we first wrote about Eden Pottery in The Bridgestone Irish Food Guide, we expressed amazement that such original and creative pottery could be so little known: our families had never even heard of Eden, and they live within a handful of miles of the shop, and asking locals exactly where the shop was only provoked bewildered head scratching. That scenario of undiscovered brilliance has already begun to change, for Heather and Phil Walton have created a new 4,000 square foot shop, exhibition space and café, and business at Eden is booming. Now, you can drive to Millisle, find the shop (not always easy: it's on Abbey Road on the way to Carrowdore Castle), have some lemon syrup cake and coffee, and buy not just their signature range, with its delicate spongeware of apples, pears, plums and lemons, its gentle blue cows and foxy hens, the plump Suffolk sheep with their mottled grey and orange-white coats, but also lots more styles, which Heather and Phil have previously been unable to put into production. This is superb work, tactile and colourful – there can be up to six colours used in a single style – and it makes even a mug of tea special. And, unlike some other spongeware, Eden Pottery is very keenly priced, so go on and buy that gift of a serving dish or a set of bowls or a platter for someone dear to you. (218 Abbey Road, Ballyfrenis ☎ 028-9186 2300 eden.pottery@virgin.net)

Moira

Restaurant
● Ivory

Club sandwiches, beef burgers, wraps and filled ciabatta are the sort of easy-going foods you will find at lunchtime in Ivory, while dinner offers pastas, noodles and a collection of steaks – sirloins, ribeye and fillet. Fries come as curly fries, chilli wedges, garlic fries and chilli fries as well as straight-forward chips. For desserts there will be classic crème brûlees, ice creams, cheese cake and crumble. The room fills up with a mixture of accents and fashions, from the lamp-tanned skinny singletons, to middle age couples (she has the steak, he toys with the fish), to the Anglo-Irish families discussing rights of way. It's a happy mix in this ready-to-wear space fringed with banquettes and colourful paintings that all feature dogs and oddly angled buildings. The staff are almost the best bit of the restaurant, with their solicitous "Are youse all right now folks?" and unselfconscious working of the room. (Main Street, Moira ☎ 028-9261 3384 – Open lunch & dinner)

Butcher
● McCartneys of Moira

Here is the action when it comes to McCartney's. It is 12.30pm in Moira, time to take some lunch in Ivory, a cute wee

restaurant just up the street. And, as you walk into the restaurant, you notice that the queue at George and Gordon McCartney's butcher's shop is actually lined up along the street, stretching long out of the door of the shop.

It is 2pm in Moira, lunch is finished, and looking over at McCartney's you have to do a double take, because the queue out the door at 12.30pm has become... an ever bigger queue out the door at 2pm.

That's the action at McCartney's. Everyone and his wife wants a slice of the pie that this crack team produce day in, day out, no matter how long they have to stay in line before choosing from amongst the exemplary foods sourced, prepared and cooked by this unstoppable crew. Of course, it is understandable why they will queue: McCartney's have the best of everything, from sausages to pies to cooked foods to the best beef and lamb you can eat. But that's not the whole story. People queue at McCartney's because they recognise that shopping here is shopping as it was meant to be, and which it can still be, thanks to the determination of this ambitious crew. Shopping should mean intelligent, informed service, stellar culinary standards, delicious foods produced to the highest specification, sold by people who are proud of their produce and proud of their skills. It should offer a sense of community, both from the people you are buying from and amongst the people buying with you.

And, if you come to McCartney's, then that is exactly what you will get. The best food, the best service, the best knowhow and knowledge, and the best feeling about supporting a community of food producers and food specialists. What mega-buck supermarket could hope to compete against the magisterial McCartney's? None. You have to feel sorry for those old supermarkets, don't you? All that money, all those profits, all that power and influence, and yet nothing they do can ever make them anything other than second best. (56-57 Main Street, Moira ☎ 028-9261 1422 www.mccartneysofmoira.co.uk)

Gastropub
● Pretty Mary's

An attractive new family pub with a pretty name, and a pretty interior fashioned from authentically scuffed architectural salvage, scrubbed wooden tables, and sprawly sofas,

this is the venue in Moira for stylish, fast favourites.
Battered cod and chips are served with mushy peas and
tartare, lasagne with more chips, and Greek salads with
fried breaded balls of feta. They take short cuts with
desserts but otherwise the food is pretty good. (86 Main
Street, Moira ☎ 028-9261 1318 – Open lunch & dinner)

Newcastle

Deli & Bistro
● Seasalt

Seasalt is a mad-busy, 40-seater on Newcastle's arcade-lined
promenade, sign-posted in pink neon and painted in pretty
pastel colours. A deli-inspired daytime menu precedes a
three-course set bistro menu in the evening. Their aims and
ideas are usually sound, with a typical meal including oriental crab salad followed by rosemary and garlic marinated
chicken with roast peppers and crisp aubergine, and then
banana and toffee meringue roulade, but summertime
demands from hordes of holidaymakers can put them under
mighty pressure, so just open your BYOB and relax and
chat about Newton Emerson's latest chucklesome brilliance
in *The Irish News*. He is brilliant, isn't he? He certainly is.
Anyone who can offend everyone is brilliant in our books.
(51 Central Promenade, Newcastle ☎ 028-4372 5027 –
Open lunch & dinner)

Restaurant
● Zest

Reasoned chaos reigns by day, when Zest is turned into a
café serving restauranty sandwiches, such as the tasty tempura chicken and mango wrap. However, the astute, youthful
owners of this rather grown-up evening restaurant demon-
strate a nous that catapults them into a league way beyond
their years. While the jolly, self-deprecating head waiter runs
the room with wry wit and brilliant sensitivity, a couple of
lads knock out plucky modern menus whose oriental lean-
ings are outweighed by locally inspired dishes. Starters such
as deep-fried Irish brie with plum and anise chutney launch-
es a very affordable set feast of smart food including succulent, herb-crusted chicken with fresh potato gnocchi, fresh

tomato and basil, or halibut with buttered cabbage mash and smoked salmon cream. Brûlées of raspberry, cheescakes of rhubarb and honey and speciality coffees follow, so make sure that BYOB includes a half of something sweet and sticky. (22-24 Main Street, Newcastle ☎ 028-4372 5757 – Open lunch & dinner)

only in ulster

irish stew

The Ulster variety is made with steak pieces instead of lamb, and predominantly potatoes - but also carrot onion and parsnip – cooked to a hot peppery slush.

Newtownards

Greengrocer
● Homegrown

Homegrown is a legend in its own demesne, a benchmark vegetable shop where you will find the best local vegetables sold at the very peak of their perfection, in a shop that shows what shopping could be and should be: local foods in a local shop for local folk. Margaret White has won the respect and custom of her devoted customers – and by devoted, we mean Devoted – by sticking to what she knows, and by being selective and astute, and helpful.A wonderful place to shop, thanks to great staff and a great selection of stuff that brims with vigour. (66b East Street, Newtownards ☎ 028-9181 8318)

Home Bakery & Coffee Shop
● Knotts Cake & Coffee Shop

An enormously successful and efficiently run coffee shop, Michael and Sharon Knott's store is a great example of Northern Ireland's thriving vernacular home bakeries.You will find a sea of silver haired, comfy-anorak-clad locals at their leisure, for Newtownards is the kind of place where Madeira and date and walnut cakes still dominate tea trays. Once you pass the bakery queues for unique griddle breads, sickly sweet 'wee buns' and fresh cream Swiss rolls, you'll join another fast-moving line for an appealing self-service counter of careful, country cooking. Squidgy sandwiches, stonking pies, and lots of home-style savoury stuff - beef olives, baked gammon and pineapple - are served alongside local renditions of fashionable salads and cliff-like chunks of sweet tarts and desserts. Tea is generally stronger than coffee, but cappuccinos are competently made, and the glass and wood-panelled vaulted ceiling makes for a light and airy café. (45 High Street, Newtownards ☎ 028-9181 9098 – Open day time)

Farm Shop
● McKee's Farm Shop

Colin McKee is a revolutionary farmer. To have established a farm shop eight years ago showed vision. To have the nerve to employ six full-time staff shows resolve. But, best of all, the produce for sale in McKee's farm shop shows someone who understands the entire holistic culture of farming and eating. Mr McKee takes it from farm to fork, with style and aplomb, and if you think farm shops are rinky-dink amateur shows, then think again: McKee's is the Harvey Nichols of farm shops, and it has a plenitude of customers who wouldn't look a jot out of place in Harvey Nicks, smart people who know what they want and who are happy to pay for the quality of food Mr McKee can offer them. The butchery counter is superb – check out that chicken mandarin, a unique and creative dish – and their own Angus beef is dark red in colour and delicious. Pork and chickens are specially reared for the shop, and from the Gloucester Old Spot pigs they make their own sweet-cure bacon. The chicken is the favourite roasting bird of choice of Caroline Workman, thanks to a skin that crisps superbly, just what you expect from a good barn-reared bird. Vegetables are colourful and fresh and have travelled only from Comber, though there are also complementary vegetables to flesh out the local foods.

But McKee's also has a USP with its cooked foods, made by the team in the kitchens behind the shop. Fantastic chicken

and broccoli bake; great cottage pie; lovely pies of chicken and beef are authentic in appearance and a culinary joy.
At a time when talk of the future of farming induces only foreboding and hand-wringing, Colin McKee has shown what farming should be about: producing and selling farm foods with skill, gastronomic appreciation and understanding, selling local high-quality foods to customers who appreciate the care taken in their production, thereby preserving the ethos of the land, of farming, and thereby preserving the culture of agriculture. An inspiring and inspirational place. (28 Holywood Road, Newtownards ☎ 028-9181 3202 www.mckeesproduce.co.uk)

Kitchenshop
● Presence Tableware

Presence is a seriously cool kitchenware shop, with lots and lots of serious stuff for serious cooks. Indeed a gift from Presence is what food lovers dream about, for all the icon brands are stocked here: Staub, Gaggia, Dualit, Wusthof Trident, Bodum, Legonart, Rosenthal, Alessi, along with lots of smart glasses and tableware that will make any kitchen the hub of the home. (37 High Street, Newtownards ☎ 028-9182 0222)

Newry

Home Bakery & Café
● The Corn Dolly Home Bakery

Sister bakery of the Warrenpoint shop and café, with more of the fine local baking and griddle breads. Join the queue of devoted locals at lunchtime to enjoy their speciality hand-cut sarnies made with their sweet-crusted batch bread. (12 Marcus Square, Newry ☎ 028-3026 0524)

Restaurant
● Graduate Restaurant

Part of Newry Institute, the food is cooked by the students. Book it through the Catering Office, it opens for lunch during the week, and dinner on Tuesday and Wednesday. Celebrated chef Raymond McArdle of the Nuremore is just one of their notable past students, and here's to you, Mrs Robinson. (Newry Institute, Newry ☎ 028-3025 9611)

Café
● Olive Coffee Co & Art House

Three floors of warehouse gallery space with a cool café at ground level, Olive serves up "formidable fudge cakes", and "moreish Malteser buns" in the space that was once, rather appropriately, a sugar store. But the food offering is not all saccharine. A crisp filo pie of spinach and goat's cheese from a menu of stews (Stroganoff or chunky Irish), salads (spicy chicken noodle or Greek feta), quiches (roast veg or cheese and onion) and sarnies (filled bagels or croissants) provide a satisfying savoury fix before you embark on the cakes. These aren't made on the premises, but you'd never know. Pear and custard cake or warm bramley apple tart have a just-baked warmth and are served with just-whipped cream. (7a Sugarhouse Quay, Newry ☎ 028-3026 7272)

Restaurant
● I Sapori

The uncannily authentic interiors of I Sapori conjure an impression of rural Italy in the midst of Newry. Unfortunately the whims of locals and the relative scarcity of the right ingredients mean that the food isn't quite so genuine. However, nor is it the travesty you find in Italian-theme restaurants elsewhere, and I Sapori is good for a cheap and cheerful night of pizza, pasta and pepper pots. There's also a very interesting all-Italian wine list. (16/17 The Mall, Newry ☎ 028-3025 2086 – Open dinner)

Portaferry

Restaurant & Hotel
● Portaferry Hotel

New days beckon for the pretty and popular Portaferry Hotel. It has been bought by a local man, Stephen Braniff, news that local folk greeted warmly, as previously they had tended not to have been habituées of the PH. Mr Braniff has the template of a classic country inn to work with, and one hopes sympathy for the building will marry with great cooking and service to create the icon destination the

Portaferry Hotel has the potential to be. (The Strand,
Portaferry ☎ 028-4272 8231 www.portaferryhotel.com –
Open lunch & dinner)

Rostrevor

Café
● Kilbroney Park Cafe

There are smashing views to be enjoyed from this café and
good homemade food – nice carrot cake, creamy coffee
cake, lasagne, sausage rolls, fresh salads – and even folk con-
certs with the Sands family some evenings. (Kilbroney Park,
Shore Road, Rostrevor ☎ 028-4173 8134
www.sabp-web.co.uk/kilbroney-park-cafe – Open day time)

Strangford

Organic Farm Shop
● Churchtown Farm Organic Farm Shop

Dale Orr can be found manning the
Churchtown Farm stall at Saturday's St
George's Market, selling the specialist meats
reared on their organic farm, including Lleyn
sheep – a breed that can be traced as far back in Ireland as
1750 – along with Angus, Shorthorn and South Devon beef.
But to see the complete range of foods from Churchtown
it's a smart idea to visit their farm shop. Here, in addition to
their beef and lamb, there is also a complete range of
organic products, from pork, bacon and chicken through
fruit and vegetables to dairy products. Dale and his dad,
John, farm 550 acres organically, and their combination of
organic agriculture with the chance to buy direct from the
farm seems to us the ideal – if not, in fact, the only – solution to the ills of global agriculture as they are impacting on
Northern Ireland. The Orrs, and a small number of other
enlightened farmers in Northern Ireland, have shown the
simple, logical way in which agriculture can gain respect, and
re-gain self-respect. (Churchtown, Co Down
☎ 028-4488 1128 – farm shop open Thursday-Sunday
9am-6pm)

Restaurant, Bar & Fish + Chip Shop

● **The Cuan Bar & Restaurant**

Enjoy good steak and chips in the restaurant, or, if the sun is shining, take a big bag of fish and chips out of the shop and enjoy the balmy tropicality of Strangford. (The Square, Strangford ☎ 028-4488 1588 www.thecuan.com – Open day time)

Guesthouse

● **Strangford Cottage**

A glamourous address in pretty Strangford, Maureen Thornton's house is chic and stylish, and makes a great base when travelling the county. (41 Castle Street, Strangford ☎ 028-4488 1208)

only in ulster

batch bread

A springy, soft, sourdough bread with a caramelised, dark chewy crust, this square loaf is ideal for the ultimate Irish doorstep sandwich of honey roast ham or egg mayo and chives. It also comes in the lighter, oversized Belfast Baps, once associated with the dockyards. Their texture is a cross between bread and croissant or brioche, and they must be eaten fresh.

Seaforde

Local Shop

● **Brennan's Garage**

Only a fool would drive past Brennan's without stopping to get a big cone of their legendary vanilla ice cream. The more adventurous will opt for either a slider, or an oyster. You don't know what an oyster is? It's not the solitary sea creature, but rather a mallowy, chewy, chocolate-dipped wafer slathered with ice cream and then made into a sweet sandwich with a second oyster shell. Restraint? Hang restraint! (149 Newcastle Road, Seaforde. ☎ 028-4481 1271)

Tea Shop
● Butterfly Farm Tea shop

Café, housed in Tropical Butterfly Farm. See page 65.
(Seaforde Demesne ☎ 028-4481 1225
www.seafordegardens.com)

only in ulster

the ulster fry

"Get the pan on!" is the cry of the returning traveller to
Northern Ireland, and the pan making the Ulster Fry is
distinguished not by its core content – sausages, rashers,
eggs, puddings, with perhaps some fried tomatoes and
some sliced mushroons – but by the breads that must be
cooked in the fatty juices that have leaked from the
bangers and bacon: sliced soda bread, and hot, fried
potato bread. Some even like to add a wee pancake.

Warrenpoint

Restaurant
● The Annahaia Brasserie @ Bennet's Bar

Michael Rath's expertly cooked, classic modern
Irish menus are the main reason for visiting The
Annahaia at Bennets, particularly on a Sunday
outing when a long lazy lunch comes at rock
bottom prices, and the family chatter in this
city-smart brasserie makes for a particularly relaxed atmosphere. A sing-song delicious crab tart with chive hollandaise,
or pretty gem Caesar with fine and crispy pancetta, will be
followed by rare and tender beef with bearnaise, or lean
veal sausages with caramelised red onion marmalade. To-
die-for desserts – such as the just cooked tarte fine with a
salt edged, butterscotchy sauce, have a svelte star-quality. In
the evening understandably, the prices go up a notch. Then
black pudding croquettes with apple chutney, red onion
marmalade and rosemary jus might preface roast marinated
chump of lamb with cannelloni beans and pistou, and a

dessert of vanilla and white chocolate rice pudding. It's just a pity, with two restaurants to his name, that Rath cannot always be in the kitchen. (Coastguard Avenue, Warrenpoint ☎ 028-4175 3222 – Open lunch & dinner)

Home Bakery & Café
● The Corn Dolly Home Bakery

A modest wee shop, famous for its batch bread with a dark caramelised crust, which they turn into tidy, tasty sandwiches in the café. (28 Church Street, Warrenpoint ☎ 028-4175 3596 – Open day time)

Restaurant & Bar
● The Duke

Ciaran Gallagher loves seafood and it shows. If he's not out on a moonlit night collecting razor clams, he'll be up the next day to see the fishermen on the pier. As well as a discerning buyer, he's an enthusiastic chef, seeking out new recipes, concentrating on good stocks and sauces. For the "I-don't-eat-fish" crowd there's a chicken Kiev and steak menu, with sauces and stuffings cooked from scratch, but really it's a sin to go there with the quality of seafood on offer. Mussel and saffron broth, crab-filled courgette flowers, and the Duke's legendary prawns with garlic, chilli, and basil cream are for starters. Follow with a heaped seafood grill of brill, hake, monkfish, prawns and crab, doused in a buttery stock of lemon, shiitake mushrooms and garlic. Or hake with braised leeks, and a velouté thickened with blended mussels. You will be stuffed to the gills but desserts are worth sacrificing. (7 Duke St, Warrenpoint ☎ 028-4175 2084, www.thedukerestaurant.com – Open dinner)

Restaurant
● Whistledown Inn Bar & Restaurant

The Whistledown marries predictable fare – chowder, surf and turf, chilli con carne – with some nice comfort dishes such as County Down lamb pie with roast parsnips, and neat bistro dishes like crab cakes with tomato and lime and coriander pesto. It's fast and fun, the coffee is OK and the restaurant is comfy. (6 Seaview, Warrenpoint ☎ 028-4174 2679 – Open dinner)

Just Across The Border

· **County Cavan**
In the *MacNean Bistro* (Blacklion 071-985 3022), Neven
Maguire produces some of the best cooking in Ireland,
and there is lovely cooking in the *Olde Post Inn*
(Cloverhill, Butler's Bridge 047-55555 www.theolde-
postinn.com)

· **County Donegal**
The Green Gate (Ardvally 074-954 1546) is for the asce-
tics and *Coxtown* (Laghey 074-973 4574 www.coxtown-
manor.com) is for the aesthete. *The Mill* (Figart,
Dunfanaghy 074-913 6985 www.themillrestaurant.com)
and *Rathmullan House* (Lough Swilly, Rathmullan 074-915
8188 www.rathmullanhouse.com) are glorious places to
eat and stay.

· **County Leitrim**
The Courthouse (Kinlough 072-42391) has friendly
Sardinian cooking and simple rooms.

· **County Louth**
In Carlinford there's *Ghan House* (Carlingford 042-937
3682, www.ghanhouse.com) and cult favourite with
weekenders) and *Fitzpatrick's* (Rock Marshall,
Jenkinstown, Dundalk 042-937 6193, www.fitzpatricks-
restaurant.com) is a popular, busy restaurant and bar.

· **County Monaghan**
Hilton Park (Scotshouse, Clones 047-56007 www.hilton-
park.ie), *Castle Leslie* (Glaslough 047-88109, www.castle-
leslie.com) & *The Nuremore* (Carrickmacross 042-966
1438 www.nuremore.com) are great weekend choices.

only in ulster

fermanagh black bacon

Made by Pat O'Doherty of Enniskillen with recipes drawn from the experiences of Fermanagh farmers, who reared pigs in the summer, and salted meat in the winter, sometimes hanging it in the chimney over the turf fire. They originally used black pigs but the name also comes from the colour of the bacon when cured.

Enniskillen

Country House & Restaurant
● Ferndale

Peter Mills is ambitious and his ambition shows both in the changes he has made to Ferndale's decor – though there is still some way to go to get the entire aesthetic right, as he acknowledges – and in his cooking, which is volatile and imaginative. He will serve a course of curried monkfish with a shot glass of lager; he will freeze a kir royale as a sorbet course, and elsewhere he takes dish apart in the modern style – salmon cured in Earl Grey tea; duck five ways; canon of lamb with confit shoulder and sweetbread beignet; a bouillabaisse risotto-style with sea bass; classy desserts such as pitch-perfect crème brulée. The cooking is spot-on, satisfying and pleasing and creative, but service needs to get up to speed to do the food justice. In a year or so, however, we reckon Ferndale has what it takes to be one of the icon places to eat and stay in Ireland. (Irvinestown Road, Enniskillen ☎ 028-6632 8374, www.ferndalecountryhouseandrestaurant.com – Open dinner & Sun lunch)

Home Bakery
● Leslie's Bakery

Leslie's is yet another of the proud artisan bakeries that survive so splendidly and successfully in Northern Ireland, producing high-quality, distinctive, regional breads for happy customers. Get your farls and fadge and millionaire's shortbread here. (10 Church St, Enniskillen ☎ 028-6632 4902)

Butcher
● O'Doherty's

Pat O'Doherty is the great alchemist of
Northern Ireland's butchers. And, like an
alchemist, he keeps his magic to himself.
There is a technique to making Mr
Doherty's legendary Fermanagh Black
Bacon, but no one save Mr Doherty knows
what that technique is. What the rest of us know is
simply that this is as singular and original a style of bacon
curing as you can get, and it is important to remember, as
pretenders to the bacon champ plinth snap at his heels, that
Mr O'Doherty was making great bacon aeons ago, and has
never faltered nor compromised on his calling.
Alchemy reigns throughout this simple shop. The smoked
lamb, the great pies and pastries, the wonderful varieties of
sausage; you name it and, like Beethoven, Mr O'Doherty has
thought about the product, thought about the process, and
then deconstructed, overhauled and reworked it to make it
just the way he wants it. For heaven's sake, this man makes
a beef burger that is unlike any other. Fortunately, he has
been rewarded with loyal customers, loyal staff, and even
loyal critics, who still can't figure out how he can make pre-
cious things from base material. (Belmore Street,
Enniskillen ☎ 028-6632 2152 www.blackbacon.com)

Restaurant
● Restaurant Number Six and Café Merlot

The pretty upstairs dining room of No.6 is used on Friday
evenings, which means it's the slightly labyrinthine and
ostentatious rere dining room of Café Merlot that is the
main focus for Gerry Russell's powerful, painterly and richly
flavourful modern cooking. Piling on the flavours is a real
signature here: tagliatelle will have a rich chorizo cream;
penne will have a Cashel Blue cream along with balsamic
red onions and an avocado salsa, whilst Mr Russell continues the Asian theme he began when he opened in
Enniskillen with dishes like Asian barbecued pork chop with
spring greens, egg noodles, lemon and soy, a mighty fusion
of flavours on one plate. The early bird dinner has proven a
big hit in recent times, offering great value for money, and
service is polite and prompt. (Blakes of the Hollow, 6
Church Street, Enniskillen ☎ 028-6632 0918 – Open lunch
& dinner)

Lisbellaw

Cookery School
● Belle Isle Cookery School

Short, jolly, hands-on, themed cookery courses (Summer Madness, Winter Wonders, and so on) where you will be chivvied along by the chirpy resident chef, Liz Moore, a directors' lunch caterer turned cookery school director, are the signature of Belle Isle. It's hard to imagine a more jaw-droppingly beautiful setting - a 470-acre lakeland estate and immaculately maintained working farm belonging to the Duke of Abercorn. The school is a converted estate cottage brought up to date with a state-of-the-art kitchen — all shiny stainless steel, granite tops and copper pots — not to mention the al fresco dining area with its patio-heater-parasol picnic tables. A maximum of ten students is permitted on each course so there is plenty of individual attention, and days are punctuated with plenty of eating and relaxing from the morning coffee and Aga croissant onwards. Those on longer courses can stay in the very smart holiday village in Belle Isle's cobbled courtyard. (Lisbellaw ☎ 028-6638 7231, www.irishcookeryschool.com)

only in ulster

boxty

Only in Fermanagh, actually. Boxty is a weighty, starchy potato cake made with a 50:50 mix of cooked mashed potatoes and grated, strained, raw potato, often eaten in the winter months, particularly at Hallowe'en. The most common variety is boiled boxty, also known as hurley, a large round loaf which is boiled whole for several hours, allowed to rest overnight, and then sliced and fried, often with bacon. Some make a quicker version of hurley, the size of a large scone, which is boiled and eaten with melted butter straight from the pot. Pancake boxty uses a more liquid mixture which is fried 'on the pan' while cake boxty, made with raisins, is baked in a tin.

Aghadowey

Organic Farm
● Culdrum Organic Farm

Brian Wallace brings his smashing organic produce to the Saturday St George's Market, where
his array of produce – everything from pak choi
to their own dry-cure bacon to fantastic organic chickens – make a mouth-watering sight, foods with heart
and soul and deliciousness that make you want to buy up
everything and take them home immediately and get started on some serious cooking. Aside from the Belfast market,
Culdrum operate a box delivery scheme, so telephone to
get signed up for weekly deliveries of sheer goodness. (31
Ballintagh Road, Aghadowey ☎ 028-7086 8991
www.culdrum.co.uk)

only in ulster

wee buns

Immensely popular, saccharine buns or squares and an
integral part of Northern Ireland's domestic and home
bakery tradition, wee buns generally consist of layers of
cake, pastry or shortbread, with sweet fillings and toppings of fruit, chocolate, toffee, jam, jelly, mint, coffee,
coconut, cream or icing. Often made up in trays, they are
also known as tray bakes.

Ballykelly

Bakery and Café
● Hunter's at the Oven Door

Part of Sean Hunter's chain of three smart home bakeries
cum cafés. One of his specialities is fruit-packed tea loves
with toasted whole hazelnuts and cherries. Enjoy them
with a cappuccino. See also page 118. (34 Main Street,
Ballykelly ☎ 028-7776 6228 – Open day time)

Castledawson

Home Bakery & Café
● Ditty's Home Bakery

Thirty years ago, Robert Ditty was introducing the croissant to Northern Ireland, after a spell spent travelling and exploring the bakeries of Brittany. Consider just what a pioneer, what a pivotal early-adapter, that makes this most singular artisan baker. The good news is that Mr Ditty has remained a pioneer and early-adapter for all of his career, endlessly refining and improving his range of breads and biscuits, tirelessly creating new products. "It really all boils down to passion," Mr Ditty explained to the food writer Lizzie Meagher when asked what it meant to be an artisan. "With artisan products, it's the people behind them as much as the product itself which counts. For the majority of artisan producers, the financial succes of the business comes second and indeed third on their list of priorities. Instead, they are motivated by quality..."

Well, pin that above the door of every food establishment in Northern Ireland, as a manifesto for achieving excellence. And excellence is what Mr Ditty achieves with every product, from smoked oat biscuits with crushed pumpkin seeds, to soda bread to the best farls and fadge you can get. Ditty's is a world-class bakery, fit to stand alongside any boulangerie or patisserie as an example of respecting breads and baking as part of a unique culture, and the shops in both Castledawson and Magherafelt, with their pristine appearance and dynamic staff, are temples of sheer goodness, tabernacles of the food culture. We are looking forward to the day, probably not so far away, when Mr Ditty becomes Minister for Food in Northern Ireland. Now, won't that be the dawning of the new artisan age? (44 Main Street, Castledawson ☎ 028-7946 8243 – Open daytime)

Restaurant & Guesthouse
● The Inn at Castledawson

Simon Toye and Kathy Tully have serious backgrounds in the restaurant business, with spells working for Nick Price and Paul Rankin in Belfast before they moved to Castledawson. Together, they seem to us to have just the right energy to create a destination address, here in the pretty Inn in the centre of the country. Ms Tully is dynamic, helpful and knowledgeable, and runs front-of-house with assured ease. Mr Toye, meanwhile, cooks with a relaxed confidence. A salad of smoked Lough Neagh eel with organic leaves and horseradish is served as a tian and dotted with blobs of chive oil, and it's a smashing dish, local foods of superb condition handled with respect. Rolled belly of pork is sweet and delicious, but it is almost eclipsed by the most perfect roast vegetables, roasted with honey and rosemary, and again the salad leaves that accompany are knock-out. Burnt orange crème caramel is right on the money, making for a perfect dinner. Service and food is tip-top, but the room needs some work to increase its restaurantness, something Tully and Toye are keenly aware of. The bedrooms are modern and provide a perfect excuse to make a night of it away from the city and the kids, something we reckon many couples will soon discover. The Inn has enormous potential, and we look forward to its development. (47 Main Street, Castledawson ☎ 028-7946 9777 www.theinnatcastledawson.com – Open lunch & dinner)

Claudy

Butcher

● **O'Kane Meats**

When Michael and Kieran O'Kane enter a butchers' competition, whether they are competing with their superlative sausages, or prepared dishes, or their awesome pies, they expect to win. And win they usually do – they grabbed the sausage-making prize in the Northern Ireland butchers' competition three times in four years up to 2004, for example. And, when they don't win, they go back to Claudy and they polish and perfect and improve their product, whatever it may be, and the following year they come back to the competition, expecting to win this time.

Is this sort of competitiveness good for business, and good for butchering? Of course it is. Butchering is a skill, and at its best it is an intensely skilled business, and the more you hone your skills, particularly as you enter the area of cooked foods as O'Kane's have done with such success in recent years, then the more you know, and the better you will be. Butchers, like athletes, need competition. Indeed, they thrive on it, and it explains why Northern Ireland's butchers are so good: these guys Want To Win.

But, it's not all competition. When the O'Kane brothers aren't competing, they are sharing knowledge via the Elite Butchers Association, they are talking at conferences to explain their modus operandi, they are passing on their experience in a practical, useful way, they are chatting with their customers and enjoying the craic. A model contemporary meat business. (Main Street, Claudy ☎ 028-7133 8944 www.okanemeats.com)

Coleraine

Delicatessen
● Belfry Deli

The Belfry is a tidy and useful wee deli and coffee house. There are lots of good jars and tins of speciality and ethnic foods for sale, and along with the good comestibles there is a nifty cheese counter. Look out especially for their own breads, which locals prize. (Church Lane, Coleraine ☎ 028-7034 2906 – Open day time)

Coffee Shop
● Ground

Good coffee and good food, good sounds, good style and good service all explain why Ground has prospered in Coleraine over the last five years, and why it has won such critical acclaim, having featured amongst the top 10 coffee shops in the UK. You can get a bowl of French onion soup and a chicken and sweet pepper sandwich for your lunch, and the sweet, light flavours of both soup and sarnie will be spot on. It's the sort of place where it is a blast to chill out at 11am with *The Guardian* and Ella Fitzgerald and a good Americano, or to recapture your equilibrium in mid-afternoon with a fresh pot of tea and a brownie to give you a blast to get you to dinner-time. There is a second store in the centre of Ballymena, on Ballymoney Street. (25 Kingsgate Street, Coleraine ☎ 028-7032 8664 www.groundcoffee.net)

Home Bakery & Café
● Hunter's at Kitty's of Coleraine

Part of Sean Hunter's chain of three bakery cafés. See page 118. (3 Church Lane, Coleraine 028-7034 2347)

only in ulster

soda farls

Substantial, chunky soft bread with a fluffy consistency made with fresh buttermilk and cooked on a hotplate or griddle, sodas need to be eaten fresh on the day they are baked or fried in the pan with bacon. They're an essential element of an Ulster fry and you'll see lots of bacon, sausage and egg sodas – a fry sandwich – in greasy spoons. They're also the base for Paddy's Pizzas with melted cheddar, bacon and tomato toppings. And they are delicious simply toasted, buttered and dolloped with home-made jam.

Restaurant
● The Watermargin

The riverside setting suggests Sydney more than Coleraine, which may explain why the big, busy Watermargin has been such a success story in Coleraine for so many years. At weekends, when the Watermargin is thronged, it's a pure blast of energy and fun, and whilst the menu veers towards the staples of Irish-style Chinese cooking, these guys are more than happy to let you into the wild stuff if you persist and tell them you want to order the real ethnic stuff. (The Boathouse, Hanover Place, Coleraine ☎ 028-7034 2222 – Open lunch & dinner)

Derry

Brasserie
● Brown's

Located in a pretty terrace of pastel-painted houses, this well-established brasserie is smartly designed with good lighting, comfortable seating, architectural foliage and the odd zebra-print panel. Ivan Browne likes to innovate but he's fed up with Thai curry-this and Asian-spiced-that. Instead he's reintroducing some long-forgotten comfort foods such as vegetable soup with dumplings, or at least giving his food a local edge. Fresh tagliatelli are coated with a vintage Irish cheddar and scallion cream. Rhubarb upside-down cake is warm and served with vanilla ice cream. Or he's giving a new slant to local ingredients – lamb with fresh oregano and Greek salad. On rare occasions dishes are complicated with one idea too many but, for the most part, you can be sure of judicious combinations in Brown's. (1 Bonds Hill ☎ 028-7134 5180 – Open lunch & dinner)

Café
● Café Artisan

Park of the plucky independent bookstore, Bookworm, Café Artisan is a warm, inviting, smoke-free, brightly painted café with worn leather reading chairs, calm classical music, pretty fresh flowers and a community ethos. You might expect a vegetarian menu, but sandwiches of roast beef and onion marmalade, bacon with brie, and plum & apple chutney, gammon and salad, sit happily alongside hummus with roast red pepper, vintage cheddar and Branston, or egg mayo and spring onion, and salad platters, which are also available in take-away boxes. Good cakes and desserts such as a creamy, grape-topped lemon cheesecake are supplied by a local community project. (18-20 Bishop Street, Derry ☎ 028-7128 2727/7128 2720)

Café
● Fiorentini's

Fiorentini's is always jammers, seemingly at every moment of the day. It might be 4pm before you walk in here for a bite to eat, whether it's a plate of chips and some Italian ice cream for the kids or just a sticky bun and a cup of tea for yourself, and the place will be thronged. Long may it run. (Clooney Terrace, Derry ☎ 028-7126 0653 – Open daytime)

Wine Bar & Restaurant
● Quay West Wine Bar & Restaurant

The best of a not-so-hot lot in Derry, Quay West has the advantage of a building with interesting architectural features. They are trying hard to offer every food option under the sun, a characteristic of many Derry city addresses, but their steak sandwich is surprisingly good – with a splurge of béarnaise, fat fries and a well-dressed salad, it turns out to be a tasty, bumper dish of food – and so you might be lucky with more elaborate dishes, but the simpler ones are the wise choice. (Boating Club Lane, Derry ☎ 028-7137 0977, www.quaywestrestaurant.com – Open lunch & dinner)

B&B
● The Saddlers House B&B

A three-storey Georgian terrace, with honey-coloured antique pine stairway and woodwork, Joan Pyne's house offers very decent budget accommodation, although single beds are the narrow, shifting kind. Good breakfasts with proper dry-cured bacon, and free-range eggs, around a shared table in the old-fashioned basement kitchen. (36 Gt James St ☎ 028-7126 9691, www.thesaddlershouse.com)

Desertmartin

Farm Shop & Charcouterie
● Moss Brook Farm Shoppe

Trevor and Irene Barclay's Moss Brook pork firm is one of the touchstones for recent devel- opments in the food culture of Northern Ireland. Back in 1999, when the price of pork had collapsed, Mr Barclay began using his land race pigs to make sausages and bacon and hams, rather than just rearing the animals for the mass market. Thanks to the St George's Market in Belfast, he quickly found an audience who loved his pork products. Since then, he has gotten better and bet- ter, he has developed his epicurean expertise, and today he arrives at the St George's Market with a grill to cook his products and a huge coffee roaster, and within minutes a queue has formed and Mr Barclay is firing on all cylinders, frying bacon, turning sausages, selling gammons and streaky bacon, brewing the coffee. For all who despair about the state of modern Irish agriculture, Mr Barclay is one of the finest examples of how going out on your own, and ignoring the commodity market, is the only way to survive and thrive. Give him a few more years, and Moss Brooke will be a pork empire, Spicy but Nicey sausages will be the nation's choice, and one smart guy will be giving masterclasses and seminars on how to triumph by being brave, and by being very good indeed. The Tom Peters of artisan pork production, that's who Mr Barclay is destined to be. (6 Durnascallon, Desertmartin ☎ 028-7963 3454)

Feeny

Guesthouse
● Drumcovitt House & Barn

Frank and Florence Sloan are kindly hosts who are likely to invite you in for tea and shortbread if you drop into Drumcovitt, even if you aren't staying.

Their well-maintained, four-storey, round-ended Georgian House, covered in Virginia creeper, also radiates warmth from the log fires and a remarkably efficient oil-fired central heating, while original shutters and warm eiderdowns keep out the prevailing winds. Still it's nice to wake up in unshuttered rooms in this stunning sweep of sheep-strewn and wooded valley, before a proper breakfast in the farmhouse kitchen. There's an espresso machine, which is always a welcome sight, and they source their sausages, blackpudding and bacon from the O'Kane brothers in nearby Claudy. However, it's not just big fries: stewed fruits and baked apples from the garden, home-made jams, and morning breads from the local homebakery all make good preparation for a stomp up the Sperrins. (704 Feeny Road ☎ 028-7778 1224 www.drumcovitt.co.uk)

Garvagh

Farm Shop
● Arkhill Farm Shop

A cottage-style shop on the Garvagh to Coleraine road, Paul Craig's farm shop specialises in organic meats and excellent eggs, which can also be found in other specialist retailers such as Pheasant's Hill in Comber. There are also home-made cakes, jams and chutneys. (25 Drumcroone Road, Garvagh ☎ 028-6655 7920)

Limavady

Home Bakery & Café
● Hunter's at the Oven Door

Once mainly a bread-producing bakery, Sean Hunter's has a fine reputation, stretching back at least 40 years, for its traditional batch breads, its honey-butter wheatens, its hotplate muffins and its buttermilk pancakes. However, it's now best known for fruit-packed tea loaves, which are chock-full of toasted whole hazelnuts and cherries, and the sweet-toothed can bite into French fancies, from the wee bun of the same name to the fine lemon and chocolate tarts. Best news is that you can accompany these with espresso and cappuccino coffees after lunches of soups, sandwiches, and Irish stews served in the café that forms part of the shop. (5-9 Market Street, Limavady ☎ 028-7772 2411)

Butcher
● Norman Hunter & Son

So, just how many butcher's shops do you know that have a quotation from John Ruskin on the wall? It isn't exactly commonplace, is it? But in Ian Hunter's shop the Ruskin quote framed on the wall just beside the butcher's counter is entirely apposite: "There is hardly anything in this world that anyone cannot make a little cheaper, and a little worse. And those that consider price alone are this man's lawful prey." So, don't be a victim of the supermarket sharks with their inferior foods. Get smart and get along to Ian Hunter's handsome and beautifully turned out store to get superb beef — sirloins hung for 4 weeks — lovely sausages and, in particular, their speciality pies that are worth the trip to Limavady alone. And in addition to the meats there are many fine foods, including an excellent cheese counter in the extended deli and bakery.

A fantastic store, and an experience the great John Ruskin would have treasured, for Ruskin regarded the state of the arts as "a visible sign of national virtue". If he switched his mind to the culinary arts, he would surely have regarded the brilliant standards of butcher's shops such as Ian Hunter's as exhibiting that "national virtue". (53-55 Main Street ☎ 028-7776 2665)

Farm Shop
● Keady Mountain Farm

Here's the proof of just how fine the organic produce of the Mullan family of Keady Mountain farm really is. Buttonhole a hard-line, food-loving friend at Saturday's St George's market, quiz them about which of the stalls are the most indispensable, and every one of them will point to the Keady Mountain farm stall. Here is where they buy their organic eggs, their organic chickens (at less than £7: what a steal!), their organic lamb – deep-dark-Burgundy red in colour and hung for two weeks – and whatever else has been prepared by the Mullan brothers to bring down to Belfast. So, we paid our £6.99, and roasted the chicken, and it was only superb, a noble bird with crisp skin, moist flesh, and whose bones made the richest stock for a risotto. What we also loved is the rapport that the customers have with the Mullan family, swapping tips and advice, recycling egg boxes, sharing chat and gossip. Now that's what we call shopping, and that's what we call farming. (Limavady ☎ 028-7776 4157)

Brasserie
● The Lime Tree

Stanley Matthews is the Limavady local hero. As long ago as 1997, the year Stanley and Maria opened up in Limavady, a correspondent was accurately summarising the key ingredients that have made The Lime Tree a success: "Friendliness, dedication and an unfailingly high standard in a frequently changing menu and an interesting wine list make each visit a wonderful gourmet experience... The Lime Tree is a joy."
Indeed it is. A modest, unpretentious place, just as you might find in provincial France, Italy or Spain, the LT looks after the locals and the locals look after it. It's classic, classy cooking – the signature dish of saddle of rabbit with warm black pudding and bacon salad; rich osso buco; Hunter's sirloin steak with black peppercorn sauce – and Mr Matthews wisely reads the conservative local palate by offering dishes cooked plainly. But, if you want a walk on the wilder side, then do try some of the culinary circumambulations this chef enjoys undertaking, for that superb Sperrin lamb is as likely to come with Moroccan spiced sauce as it is with mint sauce, and Mr Matthews shows both his flexibility and his culinary enquiry during their monthly theme evenings,

which might be Spanish cooking one month or New Orleans the next. Friendliness. Dedication. And an unfailingly high standard. Yep, that's just right for the Lime Tree. (60 Catherine Street, Limavady ☎ 028-7776 4300 www.limetreerest.com – Open dinner & Sun lunch)

Fish & Chips
● McNulty's Fish & Chips

To get the true measure of what Brian McNulty and his crew achieve in their magnificent fish and chip shop, just consider this. When samples of the new season's potato crop have been sent over from the English Fens from the Robinson family, Mr McNulty will fry up the samples, to check that they don't brown too quickly on the outside, or stay uncooked in the centre. And when the test batches are ready, Mr McNulty gets in his car, and test drives the new season's chips. After all, that is what most of his customers do, for McNulty's is a take-away only. And so, the boss checks that the chips provide the optimum experience, as you drive along in your car. Well, taking the chips along in the car is exactly what we did, travelling on from Limavady to Derry. And how were they? Superlative: crisp, dry, hot, salty, flavourful: the perfect chip. But then, whatever they do in McNulty's is benchmark. The fish is filleted and the pin bones removed by hand. The burgers are put together with the care of someone making a sculpture. And doing things with pristine care and attention to detail explains why this firm has thrived for sixty years, since first opening its doors back in 1945. The shop itself is as neat as a new pin, and so are the staff, whose appearance contributes to the haute couture character of the operation. So, do yourself a favour: take a bag of McNulty's for a test drive, today. And whilst we are at it: if cars nowadays have cup holders, which smart manufacturer will be the first to include a chip holder? We wait, anxiously. (84 Main Street, Limavady ☎ 028-7776 2148)

Maghera

Butcher
● McKee's Butchers

George McKee oversees two butcher's shops in little

Maghera, as well as selling a sizeable selection of his smashing pies and bakes to other shops in the region – you can see a good selection of them for sale in JC Stewart's in Magherafelt, for instance. The fresh meat is as fine as you would expect of an owner who rears his own cattle as well as buying local stock, but it is with their pies, scotch eggs, quiches and sausage rolls and other essentials that McKee's have created a USP for their business. Deliciously flavourful, true tasting, free of any junk, these are the sort of quality foods you can feed to the family with a clear conscience. (26 & 78 Main Street, Maghera ☎ 028-7964 2559)

only in ulster

eels

Traditionally eaten fresh at Hallowe'en, at eel dances in the local hotels and halls, brown eels from Lough Neagh and larger silver eels from the River Bann would be dipped in flour and fried quickly, or cooked slowly for a very long time, and served with onion mash. Locals recall the sight of all the women coming out of their houses with large plates dusted with flour when the 'herring' man made his delivery on Fridays - or when other men imitated his call, for entertainment. Although over 18m tonnes are exported each year, and 300 families depend on the fishery for a living, the eels are very rarely eaten locally. The Chinese community buy them in season for hot pots and steamed dishes, and Drumgooland Smoke House is hot smoking them for restaurants such as the Inn at Castledawson. Local baker Robert Ditty also recommends eating them in fresh, buttered soda, when the tender hot flesh melts the butter, and the bread is a good mop for the frying juices.

Magherafelt

Café
● Café Slice

This café is owned by the Genesis bread company, whose
breads you will find in Northen Ireland supermarkets. It's a
good stop for a quick lunch or just a snack. To see the
range of fine Genesis breads, go around the corner to JC
Stewart's, where you will find them for sale, and look out
for them in major shops and supermarkets. (11 Rainey St,
Magherafelt ☎ 028-7963 3980 – Open lunch & dinner

Home Bakery & Café
● Ditty's Home Bakery

See the entry under Castledawson for a look at Robert
Ditty's inspired creative philosophy of baking. If you don't
need the philosophy, and just want something delicious,
then walk into this gorgeous store, let the charming staff
sell you whatever it is your heart desires, and discover how
these quiet, meticulous mid-Ulster addresses show themselves to be world-class destinations to eat. A magnificent
bakery and café. (33 Rainey Street, Magherafelt
☎ 028-7963 3944 – Open day time)

only in ulster

oatcakes

Oats are the most commonly grown cereal in Ireland, and
oaten bread, made with soaked oats and baked on an
open fire, would be eaten between old and new crops of
potatoes, before griddle breads became popular.
Nowadays only Robert Ditty is making oatcakes locally.
Made with rolled oats from Co Armagh, or smoked oats,
they are light, nutty and have a just-baked crispness.

Brasserie
● Gardiner's

Sean Owens' restaurant is in a converted rugby club that
has been extensively made-over, and his menu offers

favourite mid-Ulster variants of global standards –
hummus, Caesar salad, Thai curries, spaghetti bolognaise, a
good boeuf bourguignonne. The hummus is fresh, the spag
bol has good al dente pasta and a rich meat sauce, but it's
the signature boeuf bourguignonne that gets our vote.
Portions are extremely generous, and expect a raucous
night out, especially at the weekends. (7 Garden St,
Magherafelt ☎ 028-7930 0333 — Open Dinner)

Kitchenware/Tableware
● Hatch
Situated just across from JC Stewart's, Hatch isn't exclusively a kitchenware shop – it has quite a lot of homeware for
sale as well – but it's a key spot for picking up nice things
for the kitchen and the table. (4 Union Road, Magherafelt
☎ 028-7963 2311)

Coffee Bar
● Relish
Refresh. Refuel. Relax. That's the motto of Aisling Duffy and
Tania McGeehan's hip corner coffee bar and restaurant in
the centre of town, and the girls and their team help you
achieve all those ideals with gas in the tank. It's a very slick,
very metropolitan room, with comfy banquettes and sofas,
black-clad efficient staff, and a long list of foods from breakfast to hot melts to wraps to good coffee, all of which show
care and attention to detail. A hip and stylish crowd have
already colonised Relish: no surprise there. (1 Broad Street,
Magherafelt ☎ 028-7930 1501, www.relishmagherafelt.com
– Open day time)

Supermarket
● JC Stewarts
JC Stewarts is one of the best shops in
Northern Ireland. Not only does it sell all
of the wonderful foods that you actually
want to buy and to cook and to eat –
Sprott's bacon; McKee's meats and pies;
Genesis breads; Erganagh goat's milk; Ditty's
biscuits; Portglenone beef sausages – but it offers
them for sale in what has to be the most imaginative,
artfully designed supermarket space in the entire country. It
is a pleasure to shop here, trying to make up your mind
over which of nine varieties of apple you want to buy, pick-

ing up some Hyndman's bread, buying some nice beef and lamb from the meat counter, being served by helpful, smart staff. This is a quite revolutionary store in terms of aesthetics and ergonomics, and it shows just what supermarkets can be, and what they used to be before the behemoths with their billion-pound profits came along. What Field's supermarket is to West Cork, so JC Stewart's is to mid-Ulster; a sport of nature, a true star, the best, simple as that. (1 Union Road, Magherafelt ☎ 028-7930 2930)

Restaurant and Hotel
● The Terrace Restaurant and Hotel

The people of Magherafelt enjoy well cooked, generously portioned food, with prompt drinks service, and this is exactly what the Terrace provides. Prawn Marie Rose, sirloin with peppercorn or whiskey sauce, and fresh fruit pavlova are staples, but you will also find chicken with cabbage, bacon, and thyme jus, or creamed leeks, or pork and cinnamon-spiced apples with mustard cream. Modern and global influences are creeping in with dishes such as crispy duck confit and Chinese pancakes, pasta carbonara, and chicken with sweetcorn, chilli and pineapple salsa. However, the Terrace's chef has a lot of experience, and his fusion ideas are precise and restrained. It's cosy food that perhaps requires a cosier room. (42-48 Church Street, Magherafelt ☎ 028-7963 4040, www.theterracehotel.com)

Portstewart

Butcher
● JE Toms & Sons

A small butcher's shop on the seafront at windswept and occasionally wet Portstewart, Alan Tom's shop has a particular reputation for its extensive sausage range, and also for excellent meat pies: hand us a hot steak 'n' kidney pie and we will be as happy as kids on the beach. Summertime sees large areas of the counters dedicated to a terrific range of barbecue specialities, which local holidaymakers ghoover up hungrily, all of the specialities meticulously prepared, so chill the pinot grigio and plug the iPOD into the Bose and away we go, it's party time. (46 The Promenade ☎ 028-7083 2869)

Ballygawley

Restaurant
● Ardbeg Lodge

Scalding, thin and watery cappuchinos could put off visitors to Ardbeg. Tea is the local brew and it is what you should choose here. However, the simple, competent country home cooking – mostly tray bakes, sodas, fries, lasagne, baked spuds, roast stuffed chicken or pork with lashings of gravy and tricoloured veg - is served in the pleasant scrubbed pine and tartan surroundings of firelit rooms with views of lush local land and mature trees. (32 Dungannon Road ☎ 028-8556 8517)

Castlederg

Dairy
● Erganagh Dairy

The Erganagh dairy milks its own herd of Ayrshire cows and this milk is quite widely available and it is worth hunting down in good shops through the country, for its clean, elegant lacticity is very pleasing, and the butter, butter-milk and yogurt the dairy also produce are extremely inter-esting. They also bottle sheep's milk and goat's milk, which is brought in from neighbouring farms. There are too few dis-tinctive small dairies left, so Erganagh is valuable. (29 Erganagh Road, Castederg ☎ 028-8167 0626)

Organic Delivery
● Organic Doorstep

Glenn Huey and his team set up Organic Doorstep in 2002 to market the produce from the 300 acres they farm organically. All the milk, buttermilk, cream and yoghurt they produce is certified organic, but their twice weekly delivery service to Belfast and Derry and other points in between now includes dairy products, fruit, vegetables, juices and eggs with as much as possible purchased from local produc-ers. Customers pay in advance by credit card, cheque or direct debit, and OD does all the rest. Simple. (125 Strabane Road, Castlederg ☎ 0800-783 5656 ww.organicdoorstep.net)

only in ulster

buttermilk

A by-product of churning butter on the farm, buttermilk is responsible for the distinctive flavour and texture of Northern Irish morning or griddle breads - soda farl, potato farls, and pancakes - and wheaten bread.

Goat's Cheese
● Springwell Speciality Goat's Cheese

Linda Gourlay's Springwell Speciality Goat's Cheese is a fixture of markets and food fairs throughout the North. Ms Gourlay uses the milk of her own goat herd, and makes the

cheese at the Erganagh Dairy. There are plain and flavoured varieties of the fresh cheese — plain, chive and roasted red pepper — and it's a light, fairly sweet, fairly creamy cheese that lasts for between 10 and 14 days. You will find it at the St George's Market on the Cheese Etc stall, amongst other outlets. (c/o 29 Erganagh Road, Castederg ☎ 028-8167 0626)

Cookstown

Butcher
● J Hutton & Sons

You will spot the bright striped awning of Hutton's long before you get close to this fine butcher's shop. Inside you will find a meticulously maintained glass counter offering everything from beef. lamb and pork to fruit pies and duck eggs. Hutton's have made a great success with their large range of cooked foods, so if you crave a beef olive or a dish of Irish Stew, then head for the awning on James Street. (33 James Street ☎ 028-8676 1390)

Restaurant & Bar
● Otter Lodge

Otter Lodge has a pleasant interior, which impresses with its clean and simple attitude and some nice French art exhi-

bition posters and amazingly pretty and realistic flower col-
lections. A blackboard announces the menu of the day, and
one orders whatever you feel like from the bar. There are
breaded kingprawns, cheesy garlic bread, deep-fried brie
with a mango dressing, classic prawn cocktail, lots of chick-
en dishes done every which way – kiev/Cajun/lemon and
ginger/warm smoked chicken salad and so on. Fish and meat
dishes are offered along with staples such as lasagne, and its
nicely achieved home cooking, offered at very keen prices.
Service is charming but should be more clued-up about the
food. (26 Dungannon Road ☎ 028-8676 5427
www.otterlodge.co.uk – Open lunch & dinner)

Dungannon

Farm Shop
● Cloughbane Farm Shop

Lorna and Robert Robinson are beef and lamb
farmers in the Sperrin Valley. Their aim in life is
to produce meat 'bursting with flavour' and to
leave a viable farm business to their two sons,
the farm's fourth generation. Their farm shop - a traditional,
beamed building in a lovely old courtyard - sells a full
butchery range including beef hung for 28 days from their
Aberdeen Angus-Limousin cross cattle, their own lamb, and
neighbouring farms' pork and chicken. Marinated lamb
shanks, savoury meat balls, 'traffic light' kebabs, 'chilly-willy'
stir-fries, lasagne and shepherd's pies are all made with their
own meat. Bought in hams - roasted with treacle and honey
or mustard and peppercorn - go down well with homemade salads or the concise range of fresh local vegetables
also available. And then there are apple tarts and trifles for
afters. Just wait until they get another cook on board. (160
Tanderagee Road, Dungannon ☎ 028-8775 8246,
www.cloughbanefarm.com – Open Tues-Sat 10-6)

Apple Juice
● Cumwins Apple Juice

This excellent apple juice can be found in and
around Dungannon – it's served for breakfast at
Nora Brown's Grange Lodge, for example – and
the farm also sells bramley apples and eating

apples as well as cultivated blackberries during the season.
(Cornamuckla House, 60 Bush Road ☎ 028-8772 4637)

Homeware
● The Gift Store

Beautiful woollen picnic rugs from the Foxford woollen
mills, lots of local ceramics and smart kitchen gear, and
mountains of linen tea towels, oven gloves, aprons and
other useful gifts manufactured by Ulster Weavers are available here. We liked their modern, French-inspired range
from Cally & Co, although there's nothing to beat the simply striped traditional linen glass cloths in blue, green or
red. (10 The Linen Green, Dungannon ☎ 028-8772 4004)

Guesthouse & Cookery School
● Grange Lodge

For nearly 20 years Norah Brown and her husband and
business partner, Ralph, have charmed visitors with traditional food and country hospitality at their family home.
There are few tourism awards that Grange Lodge has not
won and Nora was once the mascot for Taste of Ulster, dispatched to food shows around the world to champion her
culinary heritage. Now she runs cookery courses from the
apple-red aga of her smart country kitchen, encouraging
local housewives to get back to baking, jam-making, and preserving with fruits from Armagh fruit farms and hedgerows.
This is the kind of food that punctuates your stay for dinner
- stuffed pork and wild plum syrup, homemade meringue
and crushed strawberries - and breakfast - full fry, whiskey-
laced porridge, strawberry and rhubarb compote. Nora's
style might not be everyone's taste, but her food sure is.
(Grange Road, Dungannon ☎ 028-8778 4212)

only in ulster

fruit loaf

A sweet tea bread with a glossy, chestnut brown surface
made with dried fruits soaked in tea, glace cherries and
nuts.

Free-range Eggs
● Linda Haycock Traditional Free Range Eggs

Linda Haycock, the wife of a dairy farmer, got fed up with buying eggs and not liking them, so she bought 12 hens, and they began laying so well that she had some spare to sell. They put a sign at the end of their lane and it all went from there. People ask her if her eggs are really fresh, and she just says, "come see" and she shows them the 160 brown hens that are free to roam around the field, eating grass all day long throughout the year. And then there's the taste test. Her eggs have a richer, more traditional flavour and a distinctive bright yellow yolk. "You'll never get eggs as fresh as these in the shops", she says. When she has some spare she makes feather-light sponges, and she's a great tray-baker too. A farm worth visiting. (53 Tartlaghan Road, Bush, Dungannon ☎ 028-8772 5251)

Guest House
● Stangmore Country House

Consummate professionalism, attentive service and swaddling comfort are the main reasons Anne and Andy Brace find their guesthouse thronged with return business users. Their chatty warmth and relaxed demeanour compensates for the rather ostentatious and formal style of the interiors they have inherited, and they work very hard to make sure their menus satisfy the tourist demand for local food. Locals also love to know that they're getting food from someone they know up the road, so supper might be parsnip and bacon soup, followed by roasted rack of Cloughbane farm lamb with sweet and sour aubergine, and Sperrin Valley luxury ice-cream and homemade shortbread. Afterwards you can retire with a cup of tea to the very large telly in the gilded drawing room or to your swagged and tailed, dado-railed room. Breakfast is simple and business-like.
(65 Moy Road, Dungannon ☎ 028-8772 5600
www.stangmorecountryhouse.com)

Farmers' Market
● Tyrone Farmers' Market

Supported by an excellent website, the Dungannon Farmers' Market seems to be thriving where other markets in the province have foundered, attracting an appreciative audience for local foods produced and sold by committed local food producers. Some of the principal produceers have entries in the book on their own, people such as the Robinsons of Cloughbane Farm, or Linda Haycock, and they are abetted by other pioneers, such as Culdrum Farm, Redmond's apple juices, tray bakes from Joan Bird and lots of high quality local vegetables.

"The market provides dependable, traceable, natural food bursting with taste and wholesome goodness", they say modestly, and they are right. And, just in case you think Tesco have suddenly become enlightened philanthropists, by virtue of allowing the market to take place in their car park, do remember that research has shown that farmers' markets benefit all the retail outlets adjacent to where the market takes place. So, the producers benefit, you benefit as the shopper, and everyone else benefits, proof that the Dungannon Market model is one that must be copied throughout the Province. (Tesco car park, Dungannon ☎ 028-3752 3752 www.tyronefarmersmarket.com)

Wine Importers
● Wattle Tree Wines

Martin Forker's wine company is as boutique in style as the Australian wineries from which it sources its wines. Five small Australian wineries are the suppliers to Wattle Tree, and the list extends to just over 20 wines in total. We like the clean, fruit-driven flavours of the Montana New Wave riesling, the Gloucester Ridge sauvignon and the Eastern Peake chardonnay reserve amongst the whites, whilst the reds will be popular with those who like their reds quite sweet and full-bodied. We have praised the stupendous stickies – Aussie dessert wines – Martin sells, the RL Buller fine old muscat and the Buller fine old tokay, ever since we first drank these potent and Dionysian nectars, and they remain amongst our favourite choices for a pudding wine to match some splendid dessert. (PO Box 1475, Dungannon ☎ 028-8776 9206 info@wattletreewines.co.uk)

Fivemiletown

Creamery Cheese
● Fivemiletown Creamery

Fivemiletown produces three mild-flavoured cheeses at the dairy, with the mild Ballybrie perhaps the best known of the trio, closely followed in terms of profile and popularity by the blue-veined Ballyblue and the smoked Ballyoak. In recent times they have added Cooneen, a brie-style cheese but one made with goat's milk rather than cow's milk, to the range. Try leaving them in the fridge at not too cold a temperature for a few weeks, and see how something interesting emerges from the mild palette of flavours. It seems to us that there is infinite potential here to create one of the great Northern Ireland food brands. (14 Ballylurgan Road ☎ 028-8952 1209 www.fivemiletown.com)

Moy

Butcher
● Robert Marshall Neill Family Butcher

White-coated, white-haired, ruddy-faced butcher, Robert Neill, parks a wheelbarrow of fine muddied, tops-on carrots at the door of his general store, and serves a traditional, concise choice of handsome, unadulterated meats. His dark, marbled beef is matured a full four weeks before it is turned into tasty steak pies by his wife who runs the village bakery. A daughter works the counter too, raising eyebrows at her father's witticisms, and the banter-filled exchange that greets even newcomers, is a happy reminder of what a joy shopping for food can be. (Killyman Street, Moy ☎ 028-8778 4237)

Omagh

Local Shop
● Mr Eatwells

Joe McMahon's array of shops on Campsie Road offers just about everything a soul might need: a bakery, a butchery, a chipper and a hot food bar. You only need add in a candlestick maker, and the town would be sorted. As you would expect from a cutting-edge butcher, beautifully prepared and presented meat is only one element of the shop, and specialities such as their twenty types of sausage and highly-regarded barbecue food draw in food lovers from all over Tyrone. (16 Campsie Road ☎ 028-8224 1104)

Keep in touch with what's happening in Irish food

see our complete catalogue at
www.bridgestoneguides.com

www.bridgestoneguides.com publishes regular updates to entries listed in the Bridgestone Guides, as well as links to hundreds of good web addresses in Irish Food. There is also an on-line service for buying books.

Sign up for our website newsletter Megabytes, and we'll be sure to keep you posted.